THE FIVE
NON-NEGOTIABLES

STOP NEGOTIATING AWAY YOUR PURPOSE
AND REACH YOUR GOALS

CHELSEA DISCHINGER

THE FIVE
NON-NEGOTIABLES

STOP NEGOTIATING AWAY YOUR PURPOSE
AND REACH YOUR GOALS

CHELSEA DISCHINGER

Editor: Jessica Danger
Book Cover Design: Tyler James Carroll

Printed in the United States of America

ISBN-13: 9798848857931 (hardcover)
ISBN-13: 9798848838688 (paperback)

To my husband Michael.

I have wanted to be an author since I was ten years old and it is only because of your love and support that I have been able to make this dream come true. When you married me you promised my dad that you would never stifle my dreams. You told him that you would always let me soar and you have kept that promise well.

Thank you for believing in me and supporting me every single step of the way.

You are the wind beneath my wings.

I love you

Contents

1

My Story

"Small changes that seem unimportant at the beginning can translate into complete life transformations if they are given enough time."

-Chelsea Dischinger

I was nine months pregnant. Michael and I were so excited to have our first child, a baby girl. I was glowing with joy and expectancy. I had just quit my job to become a SAHM (stay at home mom) and although we had been married for four years, Michael and I were still in that sweet honeymoon phase.

I had spent months looking up baby name ideas and picking out all of the decorations for her pink and green nursery. We took birthing and parenting classes together. We were the epitome of prepared and life was bliss. Looking back, it is hard to think of many other times in my life that I was happier.

The Five Non-Negotiables

On April Fool's Day I was walking through the mall shopping for a birthday gift for my husband when my water broke. I wasn't sure if I had just peed myself or it was actually my water breaking so I called the doctor who told me to come in so she could run a test. It was official, I was in labor and this baby was coming.

Michael left work in a hurry and we were off to the hospital. Driving in the car I was excited, nervous and full of joy. It was almost surreal. I remember looking at Michael and saying, "Is this really happening?" He had a huge smile on his face as he nodded yes.

It was a long hard labor, but about twenty six hours later our little miracle Jordyan was born. The delivery had some complications and Jordyan needed special care for a while so we decided to stay in the hospital so we could be with her 24/7.

It was there at St. John Hospital in Tulsa, Oklahoma that I shed my first tear. Why was I crying when this was supposed to be one of the happiest moments of my life?

At first I thought it was just because I was tired, then after a few days of crying I thought maybe it was just the hormone changes in my body. When I arrived home from the hospital the tears continued and that is when someone told me about a thing called, "baby blues."

This is a common condition that new mothers can experience for the first few weeks after birth. Mothers can feel tired, moody, irritable and highly emotional among other things. Baby blues usually goes away within the first few weeks. "That's what this is, it must be the baby blues", I told myself.

The weeks and months passed by and before I knew it Jordyan was one year old and I was still crying. At this point it was no longer just the baby blues or a case of being overly tired, it had become full-blown postpartum depression.

I felt numb: numb to the world, numb to my family and numb to God. Everything was hard. Attempting to wash a few dirty dishes in the sink felt like climbing Mount Everest. Most days I just couldn't do it.

It was hard to catch my breath, I felt like I was on the verge of suffocating from the immense sadness or drowning from my disappointment. I was disappointed in myself as a mother, wife, Christian and woman.

I looked so hard for the light, but the hole I was in was dark and deep and each year it just got deeper and deeper. Although I got better at coping with the pain, it never got less severe.

The sorrow was relentless, it didn't take vacations and it showed me no mercy. Not even on the days I laid on my floor and begged for even a scrap of relief.

When Jordyan was awake I would spend all of my physical and mental energy on her, trying to make sure she was happy and had everything she needed. To be honest, I did a really good job taking care of her in the midst of my pain, but as soon as she went down for a nap I would collapse.

Tears and anger and feelings of failure were my constant companions. When I wasn't mad at myself for not being a "happy" mother I was ashamed of myself for having a hard time with motherhood when everyone else around me made it look so easy. *Women have been having babies for thousands of years and have been just fine, why is this so hard for me?*

The shame made me afraid to talk to anyone about what was going on. I had always been the happy person that was helping everyone else who was struggling. I didn't know how to ask for help for myself and I felt like I would be disappointing everyone if they found out I was struggling so much.

After hiding my struggles for a long time, I finally found the courage to reach out to two of my mom friends to talk about my depression. I remember pacing around my bedroom trying to work up the guts to call my first friend. I was so nervous that the phone was literally shaking in my hands while I was trying to explain what I was going through.

My vulnerability and plea for help was met with judgment and condemnation. Her literal reply was, "You need to stop feeling so sorry for yourself. I don't know how you could possibly be depressed when you have so much to be thankful for."

She then went on to tell me how amazing motherhood was for her. She shared all the details about her happy and exciting life as a SAHM and with each word I began to feel smaller and smaller. Obviously I must be doing something wrong, because motherhood was not going the same way for me that it was for her.

I think my brain completely shut off the conversation at that point, but I do recall her telling me she was surprised that I was depressed because she used to think I was a strong person. She told me how she used to look up to me. She seemed disappointed in me and in my weakest moment her words confirmed to me that I was weak. I hung up the phone and sobbed.

I have no idea how I found the courage to reach out to another person after that, but I called one other mom a few weeks later. She told me that my depression must be a punishment from God for sins in my life. Her advice was for me to stop sinning and beg God to forgive me and then maybe the depression would go away.

Then she went on to tell me all the damaging effects that my depression could have on my child. After that I never reached out to another person again. I decided that my depression was best kept hidden deep within me.

I isolated myself which only made things worse. My husband was the person I would confide in. Michael was amazing through this whole process. We were both so young and knew nothing about parenting or depression, but he did his very best to be there for me. Every night after work he would come home to a wife in tears.

Right after Jordyan's first birthday we found out we were pregnant again. When the pregnancy test was positive a wave of emotions flooded through my body. I was excited and happy for another precious child, but so scared that I wouldn't be able to be a good enough mom for her.

I was already struggling so much, how was I going to be able to handle another pregnancy and all the hormones involved? It was the hormones that got me in this mess in the first place and now I was about to start flooding my body with all those crazy hormones again.

When I went to my doctor for a pregnancy exam I confided in her that I was going through postpartum depression. I shared the minimum details because I was too ashamed to share more than necessary, but I needed one really important question answered.

A question that was way too important to trust Google for the answer. A question that only a real doctor who dealt with babies and moms everyday could answer. Will this second pregnancy make my depression worse, or will it help make it better?

It probably only took her three seconds to answer my question, but those three seconds felt like eternity. My future was hanging on the answer to this question. I remember holding my breath and clenching the exam table paper, crumpling it up in my fist as my heart was racing.

My mind, heart and soul was begging, praying and hoping for good news. I just needed one ray of hope to hang onto that I would make it through this and that there was light at the end of the tunnel.

She looked me in the eye and said very matter of factly, "You will probably go through worse depression with the second than you did with the first."

She went on to explain that the pressures of two babies instead of one (especially since mine were so close in age) meant less sleep, less free time to relax and less sanity. She also quoted me some stats about postpartum with the second pregnancy and how the majority of the time it got worse.

I was devastated. My doctor's words confirmed my worst nightmare. Not only was I never going to get out of this depression, but I hadn't seen the worst of it yet.

I was never sad about having another baby, I loved this baby with all my heart and I wanted her so desperately in my life, I was just afraid that I wouldn't have what it would take to be the mom she needed, the kind of mom she deserved.

The reason why my doctor's answer to my question scared me so much was because I had already been low, I mean real low. So low that I didn't think it could get lower and now my doctor was telling me that it could get lower and it would get lower.

Before my second child was born I had already spent many days planning my suicide. I never wanted my kids to get hurt and I didn't want them to be affected by this so I spent hours meticulously planning the best way that I could kill myself with the least collateral damage to my family.

I thought about waiting until thirty minutes before Michael got home from work so they would not be left home alone for too long. I wanted to do this when no one would be there to stop me and no one would be home soon enough that they could call 911 and miraculously revive me.

I stopped wearing my seatbelt in the car in hopes that I would get in a car accident and die. Every time I was alone in the car I would pray something would happen and I would die. Some days my sadness was so deep that my heart physically hurt. I thought for sure it would simply stop beating from the misery and I would die.

I never told anyone about my suicidal thoughts, I wasn't doing this for attention, I was planning on doing this for real. This wasn't a cry for help, it was the only solution I could see at the moment.

So when my doctor told me it would probably get worse I didn't know what to think. How could things possibly get worse than not wanting to live?

A few weeks after that dreadful meeting with my doctor I started bleeding. I knew something wasn't right so I went to see my doctor who told me that there were complications with my pregnancy and she didn't expect my baby to live much longer.

The placenta was detaching from my uterus and there was nothing they could do about it. I asked her how long she thought the baby would live, she told me it would be a miracle if my baby was still alive in a couple weeks.

I was so scared about the future, but in that moment something inside of me rose up. I looked that doctor in the eye and told her that I would not lose this baby, but I was going to pray for a miracle.

When we got home Michael and I put our hands on my tummy and prayed for God to save our baby. I remember trying to bargain with God telling Him that I would spend the rest of my life in depression if it meant that He would save my baby.

I loved this child in a way that I could not explain. Just like I loved Jordyan so deeply despite the depression. I didn't care what her birth was going to do to me, I just knew that my life would still be so much better with her in it.

It was at this moment that I realized that love doesn't always look the same. That just because I was struggling with depression it didn't mean that I didn't love my kids like other moms who were not depressed.

I had lost my faith in God healing me, but this mama's heart refused to stop believing for her child's healing. Each day that went by that I didn't have a miscarriage was a miracle.

We went back six weeks later and did another ultrasound and the doctor informed us that my placenta had miraculously reattached itself and the baby was perfectly fine. Her exact words were, "Had I not performed the first ultrasound myself, I never would have believed that there was ever anything wrong with your uterus in the first place." It was a complete miracle.

Several months later, our amazing little Reese was born. I had two beautiful daughters and I wanted nothing more than to give them the best life.

I messed up a lot in my life during that time of depression and I made a lot of mistakes, but somehow God answered my prayer to heal Reese and to help me be a good mom for my girls. Somehow despite the depression I got up everyday and loved on them, prayed for them and fed them the healthiest food I possibly could.

I changed every diaper when it needed changing and sang them happy kid songs and danced around the house with them. I would play with my kids for hours on the floor. In fact to this day, my most prized possession is a pair of ripped jeans. I earned these rips from the hours I spent on the floor playing with my girls. Those jeans represent hours and hours of unconditional love. Every rip resembles a day that I was sad and depressed, but I chose to put my girls before my pain and show up for them anyways. I never let them see me cry.

Looking back now I can see God's hand of grace helping me where I was too weak. At the time I thought God had left me. I didn't feel His presence or see Him moving in my life. But now I see that despite my pain, God somehow gave me the strength to be there for Jordyan and Reese.

But as soon as they went down for a nap or they went to bed for the night a wave of total darkness would set in. It was like I became a completely different person.

With each passing day I would lose a little bit more of who I was to the depression. It slowly ate away at me, first it stole my joy, then my motivation and finally my confidence. I will never forget the day when I was sitting on the back porch with my Dad while the girls were running around the yard playing and he looked at me with these concerned Dad eyes. I looked back at him and started to cry because I knew what his eyes were saying, he was worried about me.

After I was done crying my Dad gave me a big hug and asked, "What happ-ened to my strong, happy confident daughter? Where did she go?" He wasn't asking in a condemning way, but in a loving, concerned fatherly way. I looked back at him and said, "I don't know Dad, I don't know what happ-ened to her, but she is gone and she is never coming back."

When I said those words I fully believed them. I had tried everything I knew to find my old self, but she had gone AWOL and I was sure that she was gone forever. The only motivation I had in life was to be the best I could be for Jordyan and Reese and after that nothing else mattered. Not even my own life.

This dark place continued and grew and morphed over a six year time period. Each year the depression seemed to take on a new face of its own as I tried desperately to fight against it. There were many mornings that I wou-ld wake up and my pillow was soaking wet from my tears. I had been crying while I dreamed, even in my sleep I could not escape the sadness.

After living six years in depression I didn't even know who I was anymore. When I looked in the mirror I didn't recognize myself. The depression had taken a toll on my marriage, my dreams, my faith and my identity.

Finding Myself Again

Six years after I had shed that first tear in the hospital in Oklahoma the de-pression had such a tight grip on me that I knew something had to change. Something inside me just knew that it was either now or never. I could not go on living like this anymore.

I was on a trip with my Mom and the whole time my mind was racing. Should I just give up or is it possible that I could really beat this and find my old self again? Do I really have the emotional and mental energy to keep fighting this? Why would it be any different this time than all the other times I tried and failed?

The Five Non-Negotiables

I couldn't sleep, I couldn't eat, I was miserable. There was a battle going on inside me. When I got home from that trip I made a decision, I was going to hunt the old Chelsea down and bring her back. I didn't care how long it took or how hard it was going to be. I was going to keep fighting and find my way back.

I knew that there was a better version of me on the inside locked away screaming to come out and I was going on a mission to set her free. I remember crying and asking God to snap His fingers and take this depression away in an instant. This was a prayer that I had begged God to do so many times before, but He did not. Instead I believe He allowed me to go through this transformation in baby steps day-by-day because He knew I needed all the lessons I would learn along the way for the rest of my life.

I didn't need God to snap his fingers and heal my mind, I needed to learn how to control my own thoughtlife. I didn't need God to take away the sadness and give me joy, I needed to learn how to manage my emotions. I didn't need God to make everything great in a flash, I needed to learn how to find greatness in the darkest places and pull it out on my own. I needed to create new habits, new thoughts and a new identity for myself.

For the first time in years I began to have hope again and slowly I started making changes in my life. Like a good parent, God didn't do it for me, but He did lead me through it.

When you are in a hole as dark and deep as mine there is a lot of work to climb out of it. So I started doing the hard work. The work started on my knees in prayer and with my nose in the Bible at the beginning. This time though, I decided that I was going to partner with God rather than just beg Him to fix it all for me. Instead of asking Him to heal me, I asked Him what I could do to heal, what I could do to change my life and find joy again.

Scriptures like James 2:17 ..."Faith by itself, if not accompanied by action is dead" and James 1:22, "Do not only listen to the word and so deceive yourselves. Do what it says," taught me that I had a big part to play in my own life, healing and purpose. It was time for me to start taking some responsibility for my future.

I spent hours each day reading books and studying mindset and habits. I went to counseling to work out issues in my heart. I started listening to podcasts and trainings and seminars and sermons from all the experts and I began to apply their teachings to my life.

The progress was slow, not fast like I had prayed for, but the snail's pace taught me a valuable lesson: **small changes that seem unimportant at the beginning can translate into complete life transformations if they are given enough time**. I learned that I didn't have to make massive life changes overnight to change my life, I only needed to start by changing one small habit at a time.

On that trip with my mom I decided that if I was going to choose to live, then I was going to live without regrets. Before my depression I thought living without regrets meant living without making big mistakes. Just don't make the major bad choices and you are good.

I have now learned that could not be further from the truth. We all have dark seasons, hard seasons, messy seasons, failures and struggles. Those are not the things that define whether or not we truly live our lives with purpose, it is our mindsets and daily habits that do.

If we negotiate in the little things that seem inconsequential, we will grow up and realize that these were the things that mattered most. Not the big mess ups, but the little tiny negotiations we made day after day.

This book is a culmination of all the things I did to find myself again. The habits and mindsets I have learned to adopt. How I started mastering my emotions and how I dug myself out of that hole.

While I am no longer suffering from depression, I am still taking baby steps forward in my life every single day. All these habits and mindsets are crucial to keep me in a good place. I am not immune to struggles or depression or hopelessness. I must keep moving forward and be consistent. I have to keep myself in check daily and make sure my feet are on the right path.

If you are going through a hard time right now and you are trying to dig yourself out of a hole then this book was written for you. If you aren't living up to your potential and you know there is so much more inside of you that you aren't living, then this book was written for you.

If you are having a hard time reaching your goals and controlling your emotions and thoughts, then this book was written for you. If you want to take your life to the next level then this book was written for you.

I am not an expert, nor do I claim to have come up with all these ideas on my own. What I have learned to do though, is to listen to the experts and apply their wisdom in my life to help me achieve my goals. Basically, copy someone who is doing it right.

I am so grateful that you have decided to take this journey with me. May this book help you to dig out of any hole you might be stuck in and stand once again radiantly in the light!

2

The Five Non-Negotiables

"Everybody dies, but not everyone lives."

-William Wallace

There was an old man who spent his entire life dreaming of seeing the ocean. He lived in a small landlocked village, but he loved listening to the travelers and merchants passing through his humble town who would tell great tales of the deep waters. At night he would replay the stories in his head while he laid in bed listening to the sound of the waves out of a seashell he bought off a passing merchant. He could imagine the sun glistening off the water and beautiful fish swimming all around him. "One day," he said to himself, "I will go and see the ocean."

The days turned to years and the years turned to decades and before long the old man got sick. When the doctor came in to tell the old man his fate he asked the man if he could bring him anything to help make his last few days more comfortable. The old man looked at the doctor and said, "Yes, can you please bring me my seashell?" The doctor was surprised at the request, but he sent someone to retrieve the shell. Immediately the man put the shell up to his ear and as he listened to the sound of the crashing waves tears began to flow down his cheeks. The doctor asked the man what was wrong and the old man replied, "I never saw the ocean."

This story reminds me of a great quote by Marcus Aurelius that says, "It is not death that most people are afraid of, it's getting to the end of their life and realizing that they never really lived."

It is so easy to get caught up in the daily stresses of life that we don't make time for the things that matter most. If we aren't intentional, we too will end up like the old man shedding tears of regret because we never did the things we were uniquely created to do.

The Five Non-Negotiables are five very important areas of our lives where we don't want to miss our ocean. We tend to struggle to prioritize these five areas because the little choices we need to make each day to achieve success in these areas seem trivial, therefore we negotiate with them.

We know managing our finances is important and we have big financial goals, but in our day-to-day life the little $20 impulse purchases don't seem like a big deal. So we keep making minor purchases not realizing that the $20 X 100 shopping trips year after year is the reason we are in debt. We underestimate the power of our small daily choices and the effect that they have on our goals.

In order to make the necessary changes to fulfill our goals in these five areas we need to become non-negotiable in little things that have a big impact. A non-negotiable is a habit or goal in which you absolutely will not compromise. You set a goal and you stop negotiating your way out of it with excuses.

It doesn't have to be big, but it has to matter to you. It has to be something that will move your life forward in the right direction.

For example, if you want to lose fifty pounds there are probably several habits that you need to change to make this goal happen. You might need to eat differently, start exercising, start waking up early to make the time to exercise, learn new recipes and more. It would be too overwhelming to try and change all these habits immediately.

If you tried to tackle them all at once there is a good chance that you would find yourself negotiating out of your goal because it was just too hard.

A non-negotiable is one small baby step that will bring you closer to your goal. Not the only step you might need to make, but one step that is small enough that you can do it consistently without compromise until it becomes a new habit.

It is a baby step that you refuse to negotiate with. You have set the goal, you have made up your mind and you will not negotiate with it.

If you are trying to lose fifty pounds, your non-negotiable may be that you will go for a one-mile walk, five days a week. Rain or shine, you are going to show up and get your one mile walk in.

Will you lose all fifty pounds from only walking one mile each day? Probably not. You may also need to change your diet and possibly some other habits, but walking one mile a day will definitely get you headed in the right direction of taking back your health. Especially if you haven't been working out at all, then walking everyday is a big step forward.

Once you learn to no longer negotiate with walking, this one mile will become an automatic habit in your life. Going for a walk will no longer be as difficult, it just becomes something you do daily.

The absolute best benefit that you will have gained from developing the walking habit is not the weight loss. The true prize is the confidence and skill you just developed to start a new habit and stick with it until it becomes automatic.

The Five Non-Negotiables

Once you have that skill down, there is not a single habit in the world that you cannot do. At that point you can begin to build on your non-negotiable of walking with another non-negotiable. Maybe you decide to swap out your daily breakfast of donuts for oatmeal in the mornings.

Having a healthy breakfast might become your next non-negotiable. As you continue to take back control over your life and stop negotiating it away, you will start to build the life you always knew you were capable of.

As you begin to focus on the things that matter most, your life begins to naturally reorder itself. Take smoking as an example, I have talked to dozens of ex-smokers and they all tell me the same thing. After they quit smoking they couldn't stand the smell of smoke anymore. Being around the smell would make them sick.

How crazy is that? Something that they were addicted to and craved every-day of their life for thirty years has now become something they are repulsed by.

It is incredible how this small step of sticking to your non-negotiables will change your life. Your entire mindset, perspective, schedule and relationships begin to transform as you refuse to negotiate.

When I started this journey of the Five Non-Negotiables I wasn't really sure if it would work. I was a total mess. Having been beaten down mentally and emotionally from years of depression I felt like there was no way I would ever have the willpower to stop negotiating. My emotions had such a strong hold on me that it was so hard to make a choice that wasn't based on how I was feeling at that moment.

I honestly don't know how I did it other than sheer willpower and God's amazing grace helping me. I knew I was at a crossroads in life and time was passing me by and I wasn't living the life I knew I was born to live. All these small negotiations were costing me my dreams, goals and happiness.

Full transparency: I felt so disappointed in who I was because I knew that I was living below my potential. When I looked in the mirror I saw shame and regret. When I considered changing, my thoughts quickly swept in to remind me of how weak and broken I had become. The idea of not negotiating felt impossible.

Yet despite all the self hate and pain I kept hearing God gently remind me that He had big plans for me. That I could change and that it would be worth all the hard work. It was God's voice that gave me the true hope because to be honest I don't think I had any actual hope of my own left.

Finally, I dared to tiptoe into new waters and dream a bit. I wanted to reach my ocean but I wasn't really sure how so I started with a hypothesis: If I take the five most important areas of my life and build non-negotiable habits that will make these five areas constant top priority, then ultimately I would fulfill my purpose. I would have ended my life having lived out fully the most important areas of my life.

My hope was that in the end I would have lived wisely and invested my life in things that mattered and made a difference and would be fulfilling. I would see my ocean!

So I started chipping away at my list, adding one new habit at a time towards each of my five oceans: family, finances, goals, personal growth and health. Slowly, but surely my life began to change.

My days began to have a deeper, long-term focus and purpose that guided me. I started making space for the truly significant things and that is when I think I can say I began living a life of purpose. I no longer have just one compartment of my life (such as motherhood) that I live with purpose. I now live my complete life with purpose. I am actively pursuing my dreams and it feels amazing.

Living a life of the Five Non-Negotiables will help you to live out your purpose and fulfill your dreams. It will help you recognize the things that deserve your time and attention and the things that need to take a back seat.

The Five Non-Negotiables

During this journey you will learn to uncover wrong mindsets and limiting patterns that have become bad habits in your life that are holding you back. You will learn the five things in life that you must NEVER negotiate about again.

This is your life and you are responsible for it. You get to determine how you live it. Will you achieve your dreams? That is entirely up to you. Will you ever lose those twenty pounds, explore those foreign countries you long to see, start that business, be the parent you want to be? Only you can answer that question and it is not answered with your words, but with your actions.

I wrote this book to help you and me take our words, dreams and hopes and put them into action in our lives. How do I do it? How do I get started? Where do I start? What do I do when I want to give up? We are going to explore all these questions in the next few chapters.

You are so much more than a victim of your circumstances. Your life is not as limited as it seems. You have the power to make changes in your life. You are valuable, your life has a great purpose. The impossible is possible!

I promise you this is true, if you will stop believing the same lies and excuses that have been holding you back in life and begin to take real and practical steps towards achieving your dreams and building the life you were meant to live. I don't care where you are in life right now or how bleak your circumstances may seem, you can rise above it all.

Stop beating yourself up about not being where you want to be in life and start doing something about it. Stop comparing yourself to others' lives and start living your own life. Stop making excuses to stay where you are and start doing things to grow. Stop waiting for a miracle to change your life and go be your own miracle.

So what are the Five Non-Negotiables?

1. Your Goals and Dreams
2. Your Health

3.   Your Personal Growth

4.   Your Family

5.   Your Finances

It is easy to look at this list and say, "Sure I think those things are important" and then do nothing about them. We choose to continue in our life of stressful debt, poor health, struggling family relationships and utter exhaustion. Some of us continue in this pattern beating ourselves up over our lack of ability to make the necessary changes because we just don't know how to get started or how to stay motivated. We are going to talk about these things in this book.

Using the same strategies, tips and techniques that I used to heal and repair my life, we are going to work together to try and do the same for you. If I can do it, then so can you.

This book is all about making real changes, necessary changes in your life. This book is meant to jolt you out of your routine that is not fulfilling and put you in a new routine full of your unique purpose.

We are going through five important areas of our lives, but I do not want you to feel overwhelmed by trying to make too many changes at once. If you only want to work on one non-negotiable at a time that is perfectly fine.

The point is not to become perfect or get it all together in these five areas. The point is to start growing and improving in these areas. To stop neglecting and negotiating with these areas. If you can learn to stop compromising and stick with one goal, then you will be able to do it with the others.

So pace yourself and don't feel pressure to set goals for every non-negotiable at once and make sure the goals you are setting are baby steps that you can do consistently.

If you will do the assignments I give you, then by the time you are done reading this book you will have:

- A personal game plan written by you on which goals you want to reach.
- Detailed plans of how you are going to reach those goals.
- Clearly defined reasons why you want to achieve your goals.
- Back up plans to help you stay on track when life doesn't go the way you planned.
- Tools to help combat your excuses.
- And so much more.

My goal is to help you develop the necessary tools to take your life back. I am already so excited for you, the fact that you are even reading this means that the possibilities for your future are endless! You are already taking the first step towards living a life without regret. So let's get started, turn the page.

3
Are You *Really* Ready For A Change?

"It's not that some people have willpower and some don't. It's that some people are ready to change and some people are not."

-James Gordon

Are you ready for change?

Let me ask you again.

Are you REALLY ready for change?

Maybe I should say it this way: are you ready to start taking action and applying what you are going to learn? Or are you just ready to read a new book?

The Five Non-Negotiables

This is an important question to consider because if you are not ready to start making changes, then you might not be ready for this book. The reading part of the book is actually where the least amount of change will occur for you. It is in *applying* the book that the big changes will happen.

This book is not full of new information that you have never heard. **You don't need to learn new things in life right now, you need to start living out the things that you already know that you should be doing.** I am going to ask you tough questions. I know they are tough because I have asked myself the same questions.

Growing up in church there were many times I would hear a great sermon about something that I happened to be going through in that exact moment. On a Sunday morning when my pastor would speak about forgiveness it just so happened to be the exact same time I was having a hard time forgiving my friend.

While I always love hearing the perfect message for the moment, I can look back many times and recognize that while I heard the message and it rang true to my heart and convicted and challenged me, by the time I came home from church and made lunch for the family I had already forgotten all about what the pastor had said.

I heard the words and I wanted to make the appropriate changes, but I wasn't really ready to change my behavior. I wasn't *applying* anything I was learning from church to my actual life. I missed so many incredible opportunities to make small, but powerful changes because I listened, but did not take action.

People who are living out their goals, dreams and purpose are not better than you. They are not more gifted or talented than you. People who are doing better than you in life are not better than you, they are simply living out their non-negotiables. They have created a life full of habits that help them thrive and succeed in the most important areas in their lives.

The good news is that you can do the exact same thing. By simply doing the things you know you should be doing. Successful people apply knowledge, unsuccessful people do not. Honestly, it is that easy, you don't have to be a rocket scientist to live out your purpose, but simple does not always mean easy and that my friend is why not everyone does it. Not because it is too hard to know what to do, but because they think it is too hard to *actually* do.

How To Read This Book

In your hand right now is the possibility of a true life-changing experience. You are holding more than a book, you are holding a game plan for your life. A game plan that you are actually going to write out and discover through this process. I hope you begin to see it as such. This is a playbook you can use to help set yourself up for greater things.

Throughout each chapter there will be pit stops along the way called, "Your Turn." This is where you get to interact and begin applying what you are learning to your own life. This is where the magic begins, so please don't skip them. Take your time with each question and activity and be honest with yourself.

Sometimes, the "Your Turn" will be a few questions to answer and sometimes they will require you to put the book down and get up and do something. Whatever is asked of you, it is extremely important that you do it. Remember the "doing" is so much more important than the reading.

At the beginning of the book we are going to go over some basics. I don't want you to skip these chapters because you have already heard this material before or done these activities already. If you are struggling with setting and keeping goals, with living out your purpose or changing your habits then you probably need to hear this material again and do these steps again.

If you stick with me through the beginning it will all start to come together and you will be so glad you didn't skip ahead. I am taking extra time to discuss the importance of completing the activities because unless you complete them, this will just be another book you read that inspires change, but doesn't force you to make change.

Only you can decide if this book is going to be just another good read or a life transformation.

I want you to make changes in your life because your financial, spiritual, marriage, family and health situation won't change until you do. You are reading this book because you need to make some changes in your life. I want you to face the person in the mirror and recognize the changes you need to make and develop an actual game plan on how to make the changes and stick with it.

I have also split the book up into parts. Rather than list all five of the non-negotiables at once I have scattered a few very important chapters between each non-negotiable. These chapters will help you succeed at the non-negotiables.

For those of you Type A personalities it might be a bit difficult to wait to find out all the non-negotiables details, but this is a journey and trust me each and every chapter has been written for your benefit. Don't get impatient and jump ahead.

One last thing, when I started my journey of the Five Non-negotiables all five of these areas of my life were in total disarray. I was such a mess that it seemed impossible for me to get any of these areas together. I had to start small and that is exactly what I am asking you to do.

Take this journey slowly because our goal isn't just finishing a book, it is using the book to make real change in your life that lasts. If you can only do one non-negotiable at a time that is perfectly OK. Go at your own pace, all I ask is that you keep moving forward each day growing and improving.

You can't change your habits by reading a book once and agreeing with its ideas. You need to continually feed this new way of thinking and acting into your mind regularly, until new habits emerge in your life. So please take your time in reading this book and be sure to apply what you find useful to your own life as much as possible. So what do you say? How about we let the adventure begin?

Your Turn

Let's stop right here and take an honest minute. Are you actually ready to start making changes in your life? Are you willing to do the hard things and be consistent? Use the space below to answer the question. Be honest, lying to yourself won't help you.

Are you ready to start making changes?

If you are ready, why are you ready now?

Commit to spending time each day/week on this book until you have completed the entire thing. This time is sacred, treat it as such. It is time for you to invest in yourself, your family and your future.

Pull out your calendar and schedule time to consistently read and work through this book. Decide if you are going to read a little each day, every other day, once a week, whatever you decide, schedule the exact time into your calendar.

These dates are non-negotiable, so don't even think about standing me up. Write, "Now that's what I call a hot date," below once you have scheduled your dates.

4

Goal Setting

"The people who get things done, who lead, who grow and who make an impact—those people have goals."

-Seth Godin

Before we jump into our first non-negotiable, we have to set some goals. You will need this goal setting chapter for all five of the non-negotiables so please take your time and complete the whole chapter.

Our first non-negotiable will help us reach our goals, but before we can apply non-negotiable #1 which is Reviewing our Goal Daily, we have to set our goals that we are going to review. So let's jump in and get started setting goals.

We tell our kids, "You can be anything that you want to be," or "The world is yours." Yet when it comes to our own lives we don't always live what we preach. If we are completely honest when it comes to our goals and dreams we are raising our kids in more of a "do as I say not as I do" mentality. Not only is that unfortunate for our children, but it is also unfortunate for ourselves.

I get it, trust me I do: we are so dang busy trying to raise these precious kids and provide for them and manage our careers and homes that our dreams have been put on the back burner. We start to believe that living a life that includes accomplishing our dreams is only for the lucky few, but not for ordinary people like us. We have settled for a life that does not include reaching our goals and dreams because we have created a life that has prioritized other things over them.

I am not trying to say that everyone's life should always be all about their dreams and everyone should be living the dream life. That is not realistic, but what is realistic is creating time and space for your personal goals and dreams in the midst of your crazy schedule.

How To Set Goals

First off, I know that some of the things we are going to discuss about goal setting may seem basic or you may have heard them before. Remember, I am not here to teach you a bunch of new things. I am here to help you actually start doing the things that you probably already know you should be doing. What good is it to know something if you don't use the knowledge?

If you are not at a place in life where you are setting goals and reaching them consistently then, I don't really care how many times you have set goals or heard inspirational speeches or podcasts about goals, you obviously need to hear it again. You are not applying the teachings to your life, you are missing the best part.

So no whining and no skipping the process, let's do this and this time let's use the tips and tricks that I have learned along the way to actually stick with our goals and change our lives.

We are going to walk through the steps of goal setting right now. For better understanding we are going to use an example goal along the way.

Our example goal will be: I want to read more.

Step 1: Be Specific

This has been said a million times and rightfully so! If you don't know exactly what you are wanting to achieve, then how are you going to know once you have achieved it? It is also hard to create a strategy to help you reach your goal if you don't know exactly where you are trying to go.

How many books are you wanting to read? What would be the measure that you were reading more books? How would you know once you achieved it? You can't throw a desire on a piece of paper and decide that it is a goal. Goals must be specific, so you know exactly what you are trying to achieve and how to achieve it.

Instead of saying I want to read more, your goal could be: I want to read 12 books.

Reading 12 books makes a lot more sense to your brain. It is a tangible goal that you can work towards. It is no longer some obscure thought. You could get even more specific and write out exactly what 12 books you want to read. For the sake of simplifying the example I didn't go into too much detail, but when it comes to your personal goals, spare no detail.

Sometimes when we think we are lacking in motivation we are actually lacking in clarity. We don't really know what we want and therefore there is no motivation to pursue it. The more specific that you can be the more likely you will be motivated to achieve it.

Your Turn

What is one goal that you want to achieve? Take a minute to write down
here and don't forget to be specific. Your goal can be anything that you
want to accomplish, big or small. Maybe your goal right now is just
simply to finish reading this book. Whatever it is, write it down and make
it clear. What is one goal that you want to achieve?

Step 2: Be Measurable

Being specific is not enough though, your goal must also be measurable.
This means that there is a precise date that you want to accomplish the goal
by or a precise measurement by which you will know that you have achieved
your goal.

Saying you want to lose weight is not setting a goal, that is making a general
statement. Setting a goal to lose five pounds in two months is both specific
and measurable. You need to know exactly when you want to accomplish
the goal by and what will be the exact measure of its achievement.

So if my goal is to read 12 books, I would need to know the date that I
wanted to complete reading all 12 books. If I want to complete reading
these books in a year then my specific and measurable goal would be: I will
read 12 books by December 31st 20XX.

Your Turn

Now it is time to put a measurement to your goal. Is there a certain date you want to achieve your goal by or a certain amount that you want to reach? What would be the measurement that you would know you had achieved your goal?

Step 3: Know Your Why

Your "why" is the reason why you want to achieve your goal. It is your motivation, the reason driving you to make the necessary sacrifices it will take to reach your goal. It is going to take hard work and sacrifice to accomplish your goal so why are you willing to make all these sacrifices in the first place? What's in it for you?

When times get tough and you want to quit or when other things in life try to creep in and steal the valuable time you have set aside for your goal, you need to have your "why" to keep you focused and motivated.

Just as your goal should be specific, so should your why. The more specific the better. In regards to our example goal of reading 12 books by December 31, 20XX our whys might include:

- Reading other books will help me improve as a writer and being an author is my dream.
- Reading gives me a chance to be challenged and taught by some great people who I cannot learn from in person.

- Reading motivates me and makes me more productive.
- I will be so proud of myself for setting this challenging goal and sticking with it.

As you are writing your whys down you should be able to feel the excitement and passion building in your heart for this goal. This is your reason, the purpose behind the goal and that should excite you when you write it down.

Get Your Emotions Involved

Once you know exactly what you want to accomplish in detail then your emotions really start to kick in.

If you can visualize the way you will feel crossing the finish line at the end of that marathon and you can hear the crowd cheering as you run through the course, you can actually get physically excited just thinking about it even though the race might be six months away.

If you sit back and imagine how it will feel to have the warm sun touching your skin as you lay on the beach in your dream vacation spot, your heart rate will probably drop a few beats and your body will begin to relax and your emotions will go to a more peaceful state.

Having a specific goal that is so clear that you can literally emotionally experience it in your mind means that your goal is no longer some abstract idea to your brain, it is now something your brain will work towards accomplishing.

The more specific you can be and the more emotion you can assign to the goal the better.

Let's talk about the human brain for a minute so I can show you what I mean. Stick with me here through this technical jargon and it will all come together.

Behavioral and Cognitive Neuroscience Reviews has a great article that explains what happens to the brain when we set a goal.

> *"First, emotional significance is evaluated preattentively by a subcortical circuit involving the amygdala; and second, stimuli deemed emotionally significant are given priority in the competition for access to selective attention. This process involves bottom-up inputs from the amygdala as well as top-down influences from frontal lobe regions involved in goal setting and maintaining representations in working memory."[1]*

Let me break this down a little bit.

1. Your amygdala is the part of the brain where emotion comes from. Your brain assigns a level of importance to your thoughts based on the amount of emotion tied to them. The greater the emotion, the higher the priority your brain classifies that thought.

    The more specific your goal is, the more emotion that you can attach to the goal because the specifics allow you to visualize yourself achieving the goal.

2. The stimuli (thoughts) that your brain classifies as the most important, (because they have the most emotion attached to them) get selected as the thoughts that get your brain's best focus and attention.

    So the more specific your thoughts are about your goal and the more emotion you tie to it, the higher priority your brain puts on your goal. Thoughts with lesser emotion tied to them than your goal will be prioritized below your goal.

3. Your frontal lobe then gets to work on how to make this thought come to reality. Your frontal lobe is the part of the brain that works on problem solving.

    If you have a goal with deep emotion tied to it, but you haven't reached it yet, then your frontal lobe processes this as a problem. Because of the intense emotion attached to that problem, it becomes a problem that is a high priority to your brain and it must be solved. Therefore, your frontal lobe goes to work on coming up with strategies to achieve it.

4. Your frontal lobe and amygdala work together to help you create behaviors, habits and mindsets to accomplish your goal. Any other thought that is less of a priority gets pushed to the side while your brain goes to work on solving the highest level problems.

If you attach enough specifics and emotion to your goal, your brain will go to work for you to try and help you achieve it.

Spoiler Alert: I am skipping ahead here, but our first Non-Negotiable (coming up soon...) is Reviewing Your Goals Daily. One of the reasons we need to review our goals each day is because when we do, we reinforce the emotion and importance of our goal to our brain. This causes our brain to continue to classify our goal as important, therefore it gets top priority and our brain will stay focused on helping us achieve our goals.

So your thoughts can actually alter your brain to start working for you to help you achieve your goal. On the flipside, when your thoughts are negative, your thoughts can work against you towards achieving your goals.

Your "why" is where a lot of your emotional attachment to the goal comes in. A good "why" that is truly meaningful to you will bump your amygdala into overdrive by assigning a lot of emotional importance to your goal. This will then get your frontal lobe to work on figuring out how to reach the goal.

Your Turn

Using the goal you set above, take a minute now to write out your "why." Why do you want to accomplish this goal? Remember to be specific and make sure your why truly motivates you. Add as much emotion into it as you can. You want a "why" strong enough to motivate you during the times you really want to quit.

Step 4: Have An Execution Plan

You have a specific goal. ✓

You have a measurable goal. ✓

You have the reason why you want to achieve the goal. ✓

Now how are you going to achieve this goal?

This is where the execution plan comes in. If we are going to actually accomplish our example goal of reading 12 books by December 31, 20XX, then we can't keep doing the same exact things we have been doing before and still accomplish our goal. We need to create a new habit.

Maybe we need to turn off the television for thirty minutes a day and read instead, maybe while we sit on the toilet every morning we need to start reading a book instead of scrolling on our phones. Whatever you need to actually do to accomplish your goal, that is your execution plan.

The Five Non-Negotiables

This part takes some time, but it is important to have a good plan. The plan needs to be detailed, specific and realistic.

To create an execution plan you start with your end goal and work your way back. Let me give you a quick example of this.

To read 12 books by December 31st my execution plan might be:

Dec	Read book #12
Nov	Read book #11
Oct	Read book #10
Sep	Read book #9
Aug	Read book #8
Jul	Read book #7
Jun	Read book #6
May	Read book #5
Apr	Read book #4
Mar	Read book #3
Feb	Read book #2
Jan	Read book #1

Take time with your execution plan. This is where you are setting up your systems for success. If your systems are not realistic and well planned out, it will take you so much longer to reach your goal.

Your Turn

Start with the end of your goal in mind and work your way back to today. What progress do you need to make each month in order to accomplish your goal by the due date? List out the to-do's and your plan to actually do these things.

Looking at what you wrote down that you must accomplish each month, what would that mean you would have to accomplish on a weekly basis? You don't have to write out each week for every month, just write out a one week snapshot for a single month.

Here is a demonstration from our example goal using the month of January as an example.

In January I am reading a book that is 310 pages long.

January has 31 days in the month.

Therefore I need to read 70 pages per week to complete my reading goal by the end of the month.

In the space below write out what you would need to do weekly in order to reach the monthly requirement of your goal. Include all the specific tasks you need to accomplish and when and how you will do them.

Just A Little More

I know I am asking a lot of you, but hang in there just a little longer. Let's break this goal down one last time. What must we accomplish each day if we are going to reach our weekly goal of reading 70 pages per week?

That is 10 pages per day.

Breaking our goal down to the daily level allows us to easily assess if we are on track for our year end goal. If we want to read 12 books by December 3, 20XX, we can immediately know if we are on track to meet our goal by checking if we have completed our daily reading goal.

Have I read my 10 pages today? The answer to that question will tell me if I am on track to reach my goal. My goal is no longer some obscure thing out there that I am trying to reach. It is now in bite sized pieces with specific tasks and timelines assigned to them that I can measure.

All I have to do is keep following the daily steps. If I continue reaching my daily goal of 10 pages per day then I will reach my monthly goal of 1 book per month which will ultimately lead to reaching my year long goal of 12 books that year.

I don't know about you, but reading 10 pages per day seems so much more manageable than reading 12 books in a year. Breaking your goal down into daily bite sized pieces makes it so much more achievable.

You reach your goal by taking one step at a time, but the steps can't be random, they need to be planned and purposeful steps. Taking the time to plan out your steps to achieve your goals will ensure that your effort is being maximized and not wasted.

Your Turn

Use the space below to write out the last phase of your execution plan. Take your goal and break it down into daily pieces.

Stand back and look at what your daily requirements are to reach your goal. Ask yourself, are they realistic? This is important so don't just breeze through this question. Can you realistically accomplish the tasks necessary each day to reach your goal in the timeline you set?

If you cannot realistically accomplish the daily tasks you need to accomplish to read your goal in time then you need to readjust your goal. Maybe you need to move the completion date back a bit so you have more time. Maybe you need to break the goal up into smaller pieces. Just make sure that when you break your goal down into the daily tasks, those tasks are realistic.

Eliminate Roadblocks

When it comes to my execution plan, I try to eliminate as many roadblocks to my goal as possible. It is amazing how fickle we can be, just the slightest resistance when trying to reach our goals can cause us to give up.

So my execution plans always involve eliminating as much resistance to my goal as possible. Here are a few things I do to eliminate resistance for my personal goal to workout five days per week.

The Night Before My Workout

- I set out my workout clothes and make sure my AirPods are charging.
- I schedule the exact time I will do my workout tomorrow.
- I plan my exercise routine so I know exactly what I will be doing for my workout.

By eliminating the obstacle of not having my AirPods charged for my workout I have taken away the excuse that, "I can't go running without my music." Already knowing what I am going to do for my workout that day makes it much more likely to get my workout done because I no longer have the excuse that, "I just don't have enough time to plan a workout today."

Creating systems that reduce the resistance we experience to reach our goals will help us succeed especially on the days we really don't feel like doing them. The days when we are just looking for an excuse to not show up, but instead our system has us so well prepared that we can't even find an excuse if we wanted to.

Take time with your execution plan, it is a very important part of your goal setting. Take the time to think through your typical excuses and find ways to eliminate as many of them as possible.

Your Turn

What are some of the roadblocks or little resistances that you can avoid when it comes to your goal? Can you set things out the night before? Turn your phone on silent during that time so you aren't constantly interrupted?

Take time to anticipate some possible roadblocks towards reaching your goal and write down here what you are going to do ahead of time to combat and remove those barriers.

It's time to schedule in your goals. Pull out your calendar and schedule time each day to work on your goals. Set aside specific time when you will not be distracted.

Make a date with your goal and once you have scheduled all your goal dates for the first month write, "I'm dating my goals" below.

5

The Art Of Negotiation

"The only thing certain about any negotiation is that it will lead to another negotiation."

-Leigh Steinberg

Negotiating is a skill that we are practically born with. I have seen toddlers run circles around their parents using negotiation skills and admittedly sometimes been the parent who lost in a negotiation with a five-year-old. I read a quote once in regards to parenting that said, "Some days feel a little bit more like a hostage negotiation with a band of drunken crazy pirates than actual parenting."

Life is a negotiation. Every decision we make is played out as a negotiation in our minds. Should I order a large or a small latte today? Should I hit the gym or climb back into bed? Should I buy the dress or wait and see if it goes on sale?

We are constantly playing through multiple scenarios in our minds and negotiating deals that we think are best for us. Whatever we have decided is most important, is usually what wins out in the negotiation. If comfort, pleasure or immediate gratification is most important to you: then the donut will win the negotiation in your mind over the oatmeal. If achieving your goal of losing twenty pounds is more important to you: then the oatmeal will win.

This book is all about negotiation: when to negotiate and when not to. How to make better negotiations with yourself and how to reshape your thinking so that the most important things in your life are the things that win out time and time again in the negotiations in your mind.

Being a good negotiator is essential for success in life.

Bad Deals We Have Negotiated

Unfortunately, we have negotiated some bad deals with ourselves. These deals include trading healthy bodies for the convenience of processed food. We have negotiated deals where the terms included surrendering a strong financial future for having more "stuff" now. We have negotiated out of being our true selves for fitting in with the crowd. We have negotiated reaching our potential for excuses.

We have negotiated deals where the cost included giving up quality time with our spouse in exchange for media entertainment on our phones and televisions. We need to take a look at some of these deals we have negotiated, pull out the contracts and re-evaluate them. Have we made a good deal or a bad deal?

Let's take a minute to talk about some bad deals that we want to stay clear from.

Deprivation Deals

"I am never going to eat carbs again." Fill in the word "carbs" with whatever your personal vice is and I am sure you have said this statement yourself before. Many times when people decide to go on a "diet" or work on their health, they choose extreme measures. Extreme may work for a while, but soon enough the deprivation gets too hard and their minds start trying to renegotiate a new more realistic deal.

Depriving yourself in an extreme way will eventually lead to an unhealthy lack or an unhealthy binge. Your mind and body doesn't know what to do with the extreme lack so it begins to overcompensate by negotiating. Your mind begins to try and convince you to go back to the way you were before.

Have you ever tried to lose weight through the deprivation method? Absolutely no carbs, no sugar, no gluten and no calories. After a few days of starving you just can't take it anymore and you give in. It starts with one slice of bread which quickly turns into the whole loaf with extra butter.

Normally you would feel sick after eating that much, but you still aren't satisfied, you are now craving something sweet so you pull out the ice cream. One bite turns into one pint and before you know it you have fallen off the wagon often gaining back more weight than you lost.

Depriving yourself in an unhealthy manner and then negotiating your way out of your deprivation is not a recipe for success. If you want to negotiate a new deal with yourself regarding your health or in any area, don't make a deal that involves complete deprivation. Make a realistic and balanced deal that you can stick with.

Overachieving Deals

On the other end of the spectrum, for all of you overachievers, it is an equally bad negotiation when the terms force you to try and change everything at the same time. You need to make sure you negotiate a realistic set of terms that you can maintain long term.

If you were negotiating your first real estate investment contract, your seasoned mentor would not recommend taking on a huge multi-unit property. They would probably tell you to start small with your first investment and work your way up to the bigger properties so you don't end up over-extending yourself.

The same is true with your goals. Are you making small contracts that are reasonable and wise for a beginner or are you trying to be a real estate tycoon on your first deal?

Extremism might get you a jump forward towards your goal at the beginning, but ultimately it isn't sustainable and you will crash and burn with those kinds of deals. Don't make overachieving deals with yourself. Be a wise negotiator.

Copycat Deals

Negotiating a deal with yourself that will force you to try and be like someone else is not a good deal. I understand there are great mentors and leaders to look up to and emulate, but I am talking about comparison.

Looking at other's lives on social media or magazine covers and then trying to make deals with yourself that will help you become more like them and less like your true self will not serve you. Just as no two business contracts are the same, none of your contracts should be an exact replica of someone else's.

Only make real and authentic deals that will serve you uniquely. Reject all deals that pressure you to have the perfect house like Sarah or be a size zero like that supermodel you follow on Insta.

Draw a line in the sand, from now on, any deal you make with yourself will be the right deal for you, your family and your purpose.

It's Time To Renegotiate

Knowing how and when to negotiate is important. A good negotiator never goes into a negotiation without a clear idea of what they want to get out of the deal. This book is going to give you a chance to pull out those past deals you have made and re-evaluate them with a new perspective based on what matters most to you in life.

Your Turn

What are some of the deals you have negotiated with yourself that are not serving you and need to be renegotiated?

Are theses deals really giving you what you truly want for your life, or are they giving you immediate gratification? Are these deals building the financial future you want or are they just giving you permission to be irresponsible with your money? The deals you have negotiated with yourself in the past might not be serving you today.

Negotiating With Yourself

The average person's daily life is filled with negotiating with others, but the most important negotiations are the ones we have with ourselves. We make thousands of decisions every day and many of them are played out as a negotiation in our own minds. We see a new pair of shoes we want and immediately start negotiating with ourselves. The conversations goes something like this:

Oh I LOVE those shoes and I really want them.

No, I really shouldn't spend the money.

But they would go perfectly with my new shirt.

Maybe I should wait and see if they go on sale.

If I wait too long though they might be sold out or no longer have my size.

The conversation goes on and on in your mind until you finally make a decision and settle the issue. Negotiating can be exhausting to say the least. All the back and forth in your mind, the uneasiness of what to do or not do. We do this hundreds of times a day everyday. No wonder we are so mentally exhausted.

While little choices like to buy the shoes or not to buy the shoes are not a big deal, there are some big deal choices that you can make in life that will help you. The key is knowing when to negotiate and when not to.

Our negotiating skills can gain us important things in life, but if we are not wise in choosing what things are negotiable then we can end up negotiating ourselves out of what really matters. Negotiating out of eating healthy, exercising, and putting in the extra hours to get the job done right.

It is easy for our self negotiations to end in self sabotage. Using negotiation on yourself to talk yourself out of something you should be doing or into something you shouldn't be doing is only going to set you back in life and often leads to regret.

Read The Fine Print

When you purchase a house there is a lot of negotiating involved. The seller starts with a price of $350,000 and you might make an offer at $340,000. The seller then comes back and offers you $345,000. Let's just say you agree on the $345,000 price point, the negotiations are still not over.

The buyer will then proceed to have a home inspection where they might come back to the seller and try to negotiate repairs on the house being included in their purchase. The seller might then counter back. Each step in the process of purchasing a home includes more and more negotiations until the final day when the negotiating is finished and both the buyer and seller have signed the completed contracts.

At that point in time, once the final contracts are completed and the buyer has the keys in their hands they can't go back to the seller and start trying to wheel and deal again. The deal has already been done. It is finalized and there is no way the buyer or seller can change the terms.

Likewise, once we set clear, measurable and balanced goals we sign a contract with ourselves and the negotiation has ended. We did all the negotiating upfront by setting our goals and analyzing the methods and timeframe in which we are going to accomplish them.

If ever there is a time you want to negotiate it is during the process of creating the contract with yourself regarding your goal. Take your time during the negotiations, this contract will be your game plan for success so don't rush it, but once the contract is complete and all the terms have been agreed upon and the document is signed, the negotiating is over.

Being savvy in our negotiating is not just for the business world, it applies to our own life as well. For many of us, we are so used to negotiating with ourselves constantly that we don't even recognize that we are doing it. Our self talk is full of self sabotaging self negotiations. (Try saying that 5 times fast.)

As you set your non-negotiables during the course of this book please keep this in mind: they are called the NON-negotiables for a reason. That is why it is so important that you make sure they are balanced and attainable. You won't be able to keep your contract with yourself if they are not.

Of course sometimes in the midst of learning a new habit or reaching a new goal we do fail or we overestimate ourselves and our goals. That is OK, as long as you don't stay in the negotiating space. Just renegotiate your goal if you realize it is imbalanced and start again. But don't use any failures you experience along the way as an open door to begin negotiating on your consistency in that area. Instead use the wisdom you gain from failures to propel you forward in more accurate goal setting for your life.

Making A Deal Simplifies Your Life

Eliminating the option of negotiating frees you up to focus solely on accomplishing your goal instead of having internal negotiations over every distraction that comes your way.

The answer to the distraction is clear and immediate. Does it fit the criteria for reaching my goal or not? That simple evaluation will lead to a simple yes or no answer and then you can move on with your day unhindered by the distractions. You no longer need to be tossed back and forth in your mind over every bright shiny thing that comes your way.

Simplifying your decision making and thought process will actually free up a lot of your mental energy that you can now apply to focusing on accomplishing your goal. The more energy you have focused on your goal, the more likely you are to achieve it.

Fighting with yourself throughout the day and staying in a constant state of negotiation is mentally exhausting. Make up your mind once and then use all your energy to focus solely on sticking to that.

So get out your pen because you are about to write up a new contract. You are going to make some new negotiations that will change your life. I am so excited for you, I can't wait for you to get started.

Your Turn

Go back to the last chapter and take a minute to read back through your goals that you wrote down. Now is the time to double check your contract. Make sure you have done all the negotiating upfront.

Is your goal realistic, have to set up a detailed plan that you can follow consistently? Is there anything you should add or take away from your plan to help you succeed?

Once you have reevaluated your goals and whys and you are happy with the deal, sign your name here to seal the deal.

X_____

Non-Negotiable #1

Review Your Goals Daily

6

Non-Negotiable #1:
Review Your Goals Daily

"Review your goals twice everyday in order to be focused on achieving them."

-Les Brown

Have you ever set a New Year's Resolution only to completely forget about it or give up on it a month later? According to U.S. News & World Report, 80 percent of New Year's resolutions fail by February.[1] We have a tendency to set our goals with the best of intentions, but after only a matter of weeks we give up.

While there are various reasons for us bailing out on our goals, one of the main reasons is because we simply forget about them. We write them down in our journals and then tuck the journal away and neglect to look at them again.

Your Turn

Take a minute to think about the last time you set a goal and wrote it down. Where is that goal? Is it out where you can look at it everyday to remind yourself about it or is it on a piece of paper hidden somewhere?

Did you achieve that goal?

I have always been really good about writing out my goals. When I have a brief moment of inspiration or motivation, I will write my goal out in detail. The problem is that once I have the goal written down I tend to work on it for a few days and then go straight back into my pre-goal routine.

This habit of starting and stopping my goals has had a negative effect on my self-image. As soon as I would give up on the goal I would immediately start beating myself up. I would question if I had any willpower at all, what was wrong with me and would I ever actually be able to accomplish any of my dreams? The person I told myself I wanted to be and the person I was being was not the same. I started to believe I was a failure in this area and would get down on myself about it.

Your Turn

Do you usually complete the goals you set, or do you usually give up on them before you complete them?

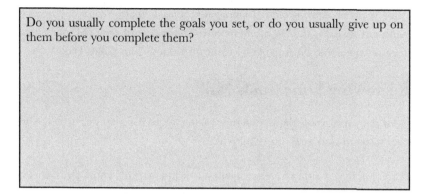

Do you usually complete the goals you set, or do you usually give up on them before you complete them?

I wish that I had realized back then that the main reason I was quitting on my goals wasn't because I didn't have the will power or I wasn't capable of being consistent, it was simply because I wasn't reviewing them each day. I wasn't reminding myself what my goal was and why I set it in the first place. Without refreshing my mind each day it was easy to forget about my goals and become unmotivated.

When it comes to actually achieving our dreams it takes a heck of a lot more than writing it down one time to make it happen. It takes hard work, sacrifice, discipline, and perseverance. If you think writing a goal down once in a notebook that gets tucked away into your dresser drawer and never looked at again is enough to make your goal magically happen then you are sadly mistaken.

If you think attending a conference that gets you all hyped up or reading a book that motivates you in the moment is enough to carry you through the times that you feel too tired to stick with it, too busy to keep dedicating time to your goal and too discouraged to have motivation to keep going, then you have missed the mark here.

Reaching a goal is hard, that is why it takes consistent, daily reminders. We need to wake up each day and remember what our goal is and why we are willing to work so hard and give up so much to achieve it. If we forget why we are doing this in the first place then there is no chance that we will keep making the necessary sacrifices to achieve it.

After years of starting and stopping my goals I finally realized I needed some sort of habit to help me remember my goals and keep me motivated. That is where Non-Negotiable #1 came in, Review Your Goals Daily.

Reviewing Your Goals Daily

Reviewing your goals daily is literally taking about two minutes each day to read through your goals and your whys.

Once you have written out your goals and whys (which I know you have already done because you did the "your turns" in the last few chapters), you need to put them somewhere that you can easily pull them out each day and read them.

It literally takes two minutes out of your day to read through a short list of one or more goals that you have, but it will make all the difference in the world.

The benefits you will get from those two minutes includes:

- Setting your intentions for the day towards reaching your goals.
- Remembering your goal.
- Planning your day around achieving your goal.
- Renewing your passion and motivation for reaching your goal.
- Getting your amygdala and frontal lobe working together to help you achieve your goal.

You must, must, must, keep your goals top of your mind EVERYDAY! This one piece of advice is a game changer.

You can't just set a goal and then hope it happens. After you set the goal you must think about it everyday and plan out how and when you are going to consistently work on your goal.

People who achieve their goals are constantly checking in with themselves, evaluating their progress and refocusing their efforts. Reviewing your goals daily is so important that you might as well not even set a goal if you aren't going to set aside time to review your progress regularly.

Taking the time to keep my goals in the front of my mind everyday and scheduling them into each day is the one thing that has taken me from constantly setting goals and never meeting them to now being able to take on multiple hard goals at the same time and succeed.

It needs to become absolutely non-negotiable that you go over your goals daily (or at least the days you're working on them)!

Strategies To Help Review My Goals

Reviewing my goals has become a part of my morning routine. After doing this for some time I came up with a few ideas to help me remember to review my goals that I want to share with you.

Set An Alarm

Twice a day I have my alarm on my phone set to remind me to check in with my goals. One of the features that I like about my phone alarm is that it allows me to label the alarm. So my morning alarm set for 6 AM can be labeled, "Wake up sleepy head" and my 12:30 PM alarm could say, "Time for lunch." I can label them anything I want.

I use this feature to label my alarms to help remind me to review my goals. For example, at 10:10 AM everyday my phone alarm starts ringing and the message that pops up says, "Review Goals."

The 10:10 alarm is to remind me to pull out my goals and read through them. I store my goals in the "notes" section of my phone. So when my "review goals" alarm goes off I open the notes section of my phone and I read my goals and whys. This reminds me of why I am going to make these tough choices towards my goals in the first place.

10:10 AM is always a precious time for me, because I often find myself distracted or caught up in "busy work" and 10:10 AM is when I am reminded and redirected to what matters most in life. These 10:10 AM pivots have been instrumental in reaching my goals each day.

Your Turn

So now it's your turn. Pull out your goals and whys that you wrote in the goal setting chapter because we are going to use them now.

Take out your phone and set an alarm to go off on each of the days that you will be working on your goals. Choose a time in the morning that you know you can stop for two minutes and review your goals. Don't do it too late in the day, because you want to be sure you have enough time to accomplish your goals that day.

Label the alarm something such as "review goals" so when it goes off your brain knows exactly what to stop and do in that moment. Once you have set your alarm, write the label of your alarm in the space below.

Now that you have the alarm set, take a minute to write out your goals and whys in a convenient place that you can easily access wherever you are. Some people put them in their phones. They either write them in the notes section of their phone or they write them in their journal and then take a picture of their journal with their phone so they can pull up the picture if they aren't at home.

Wherever you store them, just make sure you can access them even if you aren't at home during the time you are going to review them.

See, I told you to do the "your turns" in the last few chapters, I sure hope you did because you need them now! Once you have your goals and whys written somewhere convenient write, "I am going to crush my goals" below.

Night Alarm

After having the routine of my 10:10 alarm for a while I added a second alarm that goes off at 8:08 PM. I added this alarm not necessarily as a re-minder, but more as a way to evaluate how I did that day. It is a way to check in with myself and hold myself accountable.

At 8:08 PM the alarm rings and I stop for a minute to evaluate whether or not I used my time wisely that day. It is when I ask myself, "Did I reach my goals today? Is there something I did well that I want to repeat tomorrow because it is helping me succeed? Is there an area that I got too distracted or I need to double down on tomorrow?"

Any form of review or evaluation of your goals as often as possible will keep you redirecting your thoughts, habits and schedule towards the most important things in your life and away from wasting time.

Your Turn

Take your phone out again and add an evening evaluation alarm. You can label it anything you want to help remind you to check in on how you did that day with your goals. Don't set it for a time you need to be making dinner or driving your kids to practice. Make sure it is set for a time when you will be able to slow down for a minute and consider your goals. Once you have your second alarm set, write, "My goals matter to me so I make time to evaluate my progress" below.

This two minute exercise of reviewing your goals once or twice a day will probably mean the difference between you succeeding or failing at getting your priorities straight. That is how strongly I feel about this step, thus why I have made it one of the non-negotiables.

When I say daily I am encouraging you to go through these steps to review your non-negotiables every single day, but at minimum the days you have scheduled to be working on them, so if you give yourself a break on Saturday and Sunday that's fine, but Monday-Friday you should be reading them.

Since I started reviewing my goals daily I have met every single one of my goals that I have set for myself. Before then I wasn't reaching any goals.

Although this non-negotiable literally takes only a few minutes each day, it is extremely important that you do it consistently.

My Routine

To make it even simpler, let's break down one of my personal goals and I will show you exactly what I do each day to reach that goal.

10:10 am (Two Minutes)

Alarm: My alarm goes off on my phone that says "review goals." I shut off the alarm and pull up my goals and whys and read through them.

My Goal: To exercise five days a week.

My Why: When I am healthy I operate at my best, my mind is clear and my body has the energy it needs to invest in my family and dreams. If I want to reach my other goals, I need to stay healthy so I have the energy to do them. Taking time to invest in my health is one of the best uses of my time because all of my other goals and dreams depend on me being healthy. Healthy people exercise and I am a healthy person.

After reading through my goals and whys, I get to my workout if I haven't already finished it that day. Reading my why reminds me how important it is to keep my goals and renews my motivation to go workout even if I really don't feel like it that day.

8:08 pm (Five Minutes)

My alarm goes off that says "evaluation." This time instead of reading through my goals or going to the gym, I take a couple minutes to evaluate how I did that day with my health goal and set myself up for success for tomorrow.

First I start by asking myself: Did I reach my goal of working out today? If I succeeded, then I take a second to enjoy my victory and be proud of myself.

If I failed, I take a minute to think about why I failed and consider what I can do differently tomorrow.

Next, I take a quick minute to look at my calendar for tomorrow and make sure that I have scheduled my gym time. I make sure I know exactly when I am going to the gym and what I will be doing once I get there.

I don't want to show up at the gym without a game plan. I make sure I am completely prepared with everything I need to succeed at the gym tomorrow. This could mean setting out my gym clothes the night before, setting my alarm to get up early for the gym. I do whatever I can that night to be completely prepared to succeed tomorrow.

That is my entire routine right there, it is really simple.

All of these steps add up to a few minutes a day, but it can mean all the difference in the world. Your priorities and goals are worth the extra few minutes. Invest in checking in on your goals just as hard as you invest in setting them and you will see greater success.

Honesty Is The Best Policy

Sometimes we don't want to take time to evaluate our progress or efforts because we know we are not going to like what we see. You need to be honest with yourself. There will be days when you evaluate and review your goals and you feel you have come up short in an area. This is the perfect time for you to ask yourself why and learn from it and readjust.

Don't beat yourself up about it, rather see it as the perfect learning opportunity. Why do you think you didn't stay on track today? What can you do tomorrow to do a better job at staying focused? Setting goals and working towards them is a journey, we will have great days and not so great days. The point is that we keep moving forward and growing and learning from each day.

If you don't take time to review your progress then you can't learn from your mistakes the day before, so you will probably make them again tomorrow. A friend once told me a saying that has stuck with me, "God never lets you fail a test, he just keeps letting you take the same test over and over until you finally pass."

I don't know about you, but I am so tired of taking the same tests over and over in life. I am tired of setting goals and never achieving them and being disappointed in myself because I am not making the right things a priority in my life. I am ready to move forward, make progress and grow.

So much of achieving our goals is in the mind. We need to keep our mind on board with our dreams in order to succeed and reviewing our goals keeps our mind in the game with us.

The reason I have listed this non-negotiable as the first of the five in this book is because for the rest of the non-negotiables you will need to set goals to achieve them. This is where it all starts.

It is the best feeling in the world when you know that you can do anything you set your mind to. Not just because someone told you so, but because you have the tools and drive to actually accomplish anything in life. You know it because you have proven it to yourself by achieving goal after goal.

You can finally start achieving your goals, I promise you can do this. Even if you were like me, a person who was in the depths of deep depression and kept setting goals that they never reached. You can change this about yourself, but if you do not take this chapter seriously because of how simple this step of reviewing and checking in with your goals daily is, then you may not have the success you desire and that would be devastating because we are talking about your life here. This book is about five important areas in your life, these are important life-changing goals. You don't want to let yourself down in any one of these areas.

The Five Non-Negotiables

It's time to stop just setting goals and start actually achieving them. We have to stop breaking promises that we make to ourselves. We shrug it off like it is no big deal, because after all, it was only a promise to ourselves. It's not like we hurt someone else's feelings or broke a promise to our kids. But the truth is we are letting ourselves down and if we can't show up for our own life, how do we expect to be able to show up for others around us? Taking a few minutes to review your goals each day will help you keep your commitment to yourself and that sounds like a good trade off to me.

7

The Interruption

"Sometimes the smallest step in the right direction ends up being the biggest step of you life. Tiptoe if you must, but take a step"
                                                                    -Naeem Callaway

I know we are at the point in the book where we are finally discussing the Five Non-Negotiables and you are probably ready to move on to Non-Negotiable #2, but as I mentioned before, we are going to take a little detour.

Squeezed in between each non-negotiable are some important chapters that are designed to help you stick with your non-negotiables. Making these changes isn't easy and I want to give you as many tools as I can to help you succeed.

How do you keep your non-negotiables when you don't have any motivation? What excuses are holding you back? How can you stick with a routine when life keeps throwing you curveballs? Embarrassing stories about my life. These are all very important topics that are scattered in between the non-negotiables.

Ok so maybe the embarrassing stories about me aren't all that important, but hopefully they will bring a smile to your face.

Don't worry, I promise that we will get through all five of the non-negotiables. We are just taking a bit of an indirect route to get there.

I want you to have some breathing room in between each non-negotiable so you have time to think through them and start making the necessary changes to your life before we jump right into the next one.

You don't need to rush through this book, take your time and give yourself permission to go at your own pace. If you need to tackle one non-negotiable at a time that is perfectly fine. Just keep working on the non-negotiable until you are ready to move onto the next one.

Remember, you are not trying to be perfect. You are choosing a small reasonable goal that you know will improve your life. Then you are building habits, mindsets and systems to help you stop negotiating with that goal until it becomes a part of who you are and changes your life for the better. We are trying to learn to reach our goals and improve step by step.

So without further ado, let's start talking about habits.

8

Habits

"You will never change your life until you change something you do daily."

-John Maxwell

You are who you are today as a result of the choices you have made. I know we don't like to admit that we are responsible for where we are in life. It is much easier to blame others or our circumstances, but the truth is that the small choices that you have made each day in your life have led you to this point.

Most of these small choices have been habits.

What Is A Habit?

A habit is something you do consistently. Often our habits are so routine that we no longer even recognize when we are doing them.

The Power Of A Habit

Habits are small in size, but the repetitive nature of the habit is what gives them so much power to shape our lives. Eating junk food every once in a while is no big deal, eating junk food every day will cause you to get sick.

If you have a habit of eating unhealthy you will be unhealthy because you are choosing unhealthy food for your body over and over again. It's not occasional, it's habitual.

Once you allow something to become a habit you are allowing that thing to have power in your life and shape your future.

Did you know that 40-45% of your day is made up of habits?[1]

That is almost half of your daily life.

STOP.

Think about that statement for a minute.

A habit is a small thing with huge consequences. The good news is that you don't have to make a HUGE change in your life in order to make a HUGE change in your life. Meaning: habits are so powerful that by simply changing one small habit you can literally change an entire area of your life.

You must be patient with yourself though, because habits don't change overnight. The key is to not give up before your new routine has become a new habit.

Results Take Time

A father gave his two daughters each a pot with some soil and one single seed buried inside. He told his daughters to water the seed everyday so that their plant would grow big and strong. The younger daughter asked, "What type of plant is this?" The father said, "You will have to water it everyday and when it grows you will find out."

Both girls were excited to discover what kind of plant they had been given so they diligently watered the seed everyday. After a year the younger daughter began to doubt the father. "She went to him and said, "I don't think you put a seed in our pots. Maybe you forgot, or maybe this is just a trick." But the father encouraged her to keep watering the pot.

As the second year passed by there was still no sign of a plant. The younger daughter began to complain again, "This is pointless," she would say. "There is nothing in our pots." The father encouraged her again, "Just keep watering the pot."

The third year passed by and at this point the younger daughter was furious. She went to her father and said, "Father, I have done everything you have asked. For three straight years I have watered this pot and nothing has grown. Not even a sprout. Why have you asked us to water this pot if there is nothing inside it?" The father just encouraged her to keep watering the pot.

In the fourth year the younger daughter decided to give up. "What is the point? There is nothing in this pot and I am wasting my time watering the dirt everyday." But the older daughter continued to water her pot.

One morning during the fifth year when the older daughter went to water her pot she saw that a little tiny sprout had appeared. She couldn't believe it, there really was a seed inside that pot the entire time.

When the older daughter came back the next day to water the sprout, the tiny baby sprout had grown to be two feet tall. She was amazed. The older daughter came back day after day to water the plant and within six weeks it had grown to be ninety feet tall.

The younger daughter went to her pot and looked and there was still nothing. Angry and confused, she dug her hand in the soil of her pot to see if she could find a seed. But there was no seed, what she found instead was an extensive root system that had started growing deep within the pot.

The Five Non-Negotiables

The seed was in the pot the entire time, but the plant had to spend the first five years growing its root system under the soil. Without that extensive root system the plant would not have enough stability to support the growth of ninety feet in six weeks.

Both sisters had been given a bamboo seed, but only the sister who didn't give up watering it got to see the miracle of the amazing growth of the bamboo.

We can't give up on our habits because they seem insignificant, because they aren't producing a ninety foot bamboo tree in six weeks. If you start going to the gym on Monday, you won't be in shape by Friday. It can take weeks or months to get in shape. If you start guitar lessons today, it could be years before you become really good at it.

This can discourage us from staying consistent with our new habits. We need to recognize the value of our small habits each day even if we can't see them sprouting results yet. Don't underestimate your habits, both good and bad because one day they will produce something big in your life.

When we see people and they look like they are ninety feet tall, succeeding in their families and finances and goals, we only see the part of their growth that took six weeks. We weren't there with them for the first five years that they continued to water the seed even though they couldn't see any results.

Our dreams are hidden deep within us. God puts them there so that they can grow their roots deep within us and then when the time finally comes for us to sprout we have the character and habits and mindsets we need to hold up all ninety feet of us.

Your Turn

What habits have you tried to change, but you have not seen the results you wanted quick enough so you gave up?

Do you struggle to remain consistent when you aren't seeing any results?

How To Change Your Habits
Taking Baby Steps

Don't despise small beginnings, give your seed time to grow deep strong roots. Taking one small step in the right direction can have a big impact on your goal. The step I recommend is changing one small habit at a time so you don't become overwhelmed. These baby successes then make you hungry and motivated for more changes. As you tackle your habits one-by-one, eventually you will have built a life full of the habits that help you reach your goals.

I love this quote by Tom Hiddlestone, "You keep putting one foot in front of the other and then one day you look back and see that you have climbed a mountain." Success and transformation that is lasting doesn't just come from huge jumps and strides. It comes from small baby steps day by day. You are growing your self discipline and good habit muscles.

The fact that habits can be difficult to change and seemingly small, means that habits are often at the bottom of our list of things to tackle in our lives.

The Five Non-Negotiables

I had someone tell me that by simply changing their habit of drinking three cans of soda each day to water instead, they lost 20 pounds. They didn't change a single other thing about their diet, just that one habit. Do not underestimate the power of your habits! Your habits shape your life and if you want more power over your daily life, start by changing a single habit.

That is why we need to take the time to examine our habits when trying to make some significant changes in our lives. Changing one habit can also have a rippling effect in your life giving you the drive to continue to make additional positive changes in your other habits.

I love the way that James Clear talks about habits in his book *Atomic Habits*. He says, ..." the quality of our lives depends on the quality of our habits. With the same habits, you'll end up with the same results. But with better habits, anything is possible."

The person who lost 20 pounds by simply changing their soda habit became so inspired by her new body that she wanted to keep it going. She ended up joining a gym and losing another 20 pounds as well as getting off her blood pressure medications and having so much more energy to enjoy her life.

Don't get fooled into believing that you have to be capable of making one huge change all at once in order to change your life.

It is so easy to get caught up in the big life changing moments or successes and then compare every other step we make in life against them. Those big moments don't happen everyday. Most days it's small steps and small progress. Then when we look back a year later we won't believe how far we have come.

Your Turn

What is a habit that you would like to change?

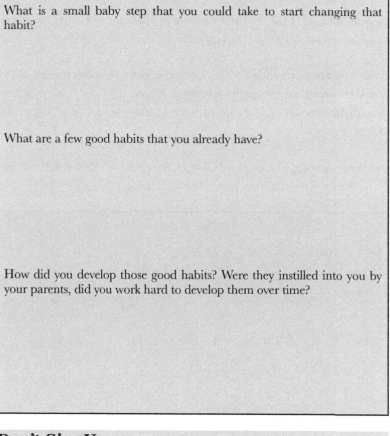

What is a small baby step that you could take to start changing that habit?

What are a few good habits that you already have?

How did you develop those good habits? Were they instilled into you by your parents, did you work hard to develop them over time?

Don't Give Up

I am definitely still climbing my mountain when it comes to these non-negotiables, but the good news is I am not stuck at the bottom anymore watching everyone else climb their mountains. I am on my own adventure, my own journey now. I am too busy climbing to compare my progress with others and too focused on getting one foot in front of the other in this rocky unknown terrain to stress out about how far I still have to go to get to the top. Right now I am just trying to keep moving.

I haven't made it as far as I wish I had, but thank God I am not the same person that I was at this time a few years ago. I have grown. I am getting better each day at growing and not quitting.

Just keep moving, don't give up. No matter how small the progress, keep pushing forward. One hundred small steps this year will equal one giant leap forward in your goals. You can do it!

It starts to get a little easier when you begin to see positive changes. When you start losing the weight or paying off those bills, but you must have enough drive to pull you forward each day even when you see no immediate changes.

Just keep watering your plant whether or not you see a sprout and one day you will have grown a ninety foot tall plant.

Your Turn

Do you struggle with giving up easily?

What is the reason why you tend to give up?

Routine

Our goals show us where we want to go, but our routine is the daily habits that will get us there. Earlier in the book we set goals so we can know exactly where we want to go in life and who we want to become. It is important to have a clear vision of our goals, but vision is not enough. We must take the necessary actions each day to turn our vision into a reality.

That is where our habits come in. Our habits are our routines. We need to set up routines that lead us to success in our goals. You need to put just as much effort, if not more, into your daily routine than into setting the goal.

At their core, our goals usually define who we want to become as a person. Our goal might be to lose fifty pounds, but what we really want is to become a healthy person. The only way we are going to lose those fifty pounds and keep them off for the long term is to actually become a healthy person.

This means we have to develop the same habits that a healthy person would have. Changing our habits changes who we are as a person. Our routines are who we ultimately become. We need to spend time developing habits that lead us to our goals and ultimately lead us to becoming the person we want to be.

Your habits will determine whether or not you reach your goal.

Consider two people with the same goal, we will call them Sarah and Betty. They each want to have their own successful company. They both spent a long time writing out their goals and whys. They posted them somewhere that they can see them everyday and dream about the day they will finally own their own company.

In order to accomplish her goal, Sarah makes a slight change to her evening routine. She used to watch TV every night after work until she fell asleep. She has now substituted one hour of TV watching for one hour of working on her business. She still gets to fall asleep each night to her favorite shows, but she spends one hour of that time on her goal first before she turns on the TV. In two years Sarah has a product line, website and has hired her first two employees.

Now let's talk about Betty. She spent the exact same amount of time as Sarah did writing out her goals and whys and she posted them on her bathroom wall where she reads them in the morning while she is brushing her teeth.

The Five Non-Negotiables

Where Betty differs from Sarah is that Betty doesn't change any of her habits. Although she posted her goals on the bathroom wall, the sticky note soon falls off and she forgets to replace it because she isn't really thinking about her goal much anyways. She continues to spend her time the same way she did before she set her goal of being a business owner.

When Betty runs into Sarah she is amazed at how far Sarah has come along with her goal. She assumes that Sarah must have made some major life changes or had some sort of miracle helper come her way and open the door for her success.

Betty wants to know the secret to Sarah's success so she asks her what she did. Sarah simply answers, "I changed one habit in my life." Betty is astounded and just can't believe that Sarah only needed to change one habit.

Betty goes home in disbelief and continues to keep dreaming and wishing, but not making any changes to her own habits because a change that small just doesn't seem like it will have any impact.

Here are two people with the same goal, but one created a habit that led her to win the other kept dreaming and made no changes.

Your Turn

Who are you in this story? Are you Sarah who is making changes in your habits or are you Betty? Are you the person who has dreams, but never makes any changes to accomplish them? Be honest here.

This is not a question meant to evoke guilt. Guilt is no good. I don't want you to feel guilty, I want you to feel inspired. Inspired that one small change can make a difference in your life.

Inspired to know that you don't have to be perfect or have five free hours a day to make an important change in your life.

Inspired enough to give one small change a consistent try.

Let the truth ring here and don't let the truth become an emotional baseball bat that beats you down. Instead let the truth spur you into action so that when you look back on this time next year you can smile and say, "Wow, I have changed so much in only one year."

This Is Your Life And Your Story

I am not going to sugarcoat it. It takes a lot of work to change a habit and in this book we are diving into five different areas of our lives that might have unhealthy habits, so please don't feel you need to rush through this book or master or even tackle all five at one time. Start with one habit and master that before moving on.

Take your time and don't feel pressure to perfect these five areas. Our goal is to improve in these five areas, not to become perfect in them. Making one small step forward is something you should be really proud of.

Once again I want to repeat that this is your book to write, your journey and your life so if you decide the best plan of action for you is to only take on one area of the Five Non-Negotiables at a time that is perfectly fine. You get to determine the pace of this journey. Do what is manageable for you, just keep doing is all I ask.

9
Start Neglecting Things

"Things which matter most must never be at the mercy of things which matter least"

-Goethe

There once was an incredibly talented professional pianist. Her music was so beautiful it would bring an entire audience to tears. The way her fingers moved across the piano was simultaneously astonishing and mesmerizing.

One day after putting on a beautiful concert, a man who was a fellow pianist snuck backstage because he had to know the answer to one simple question. In all his years, he had never seen anyone play with such precision and grace. "Excuse me miss", he said as he tapped the girl on the shoulder. She turned around as he continued, "It was as if an angel from heaven was playing herself. Please, you must tell me what is your secret to becoming such an accomplished pianist?"

Her answer surprised the man. "Neglect!" she said. "Neglect?" asked the puzzled man, "That is your secret?" "Yes" said the girl, "I simply neglected everything else that did not help me become a better pianist."

People who live with a purpose were not just born living that way, they discovered their purpose and then said "No" to other things in their life that did not align with their purpose.

Sometimes our own lives could use some selective neglect. Neglect of the TV, internet, shopping and sometimes even work in order to help us reach our goals. But we don't like neglect, neglect hurts. It doesn't allow us to fulfill our late night cravings, forces us out of our comfort zones, makes us not buy the new dress or say no to that extra scoop of ice cream. It means we can't let our emotions decide for us. Heck, it means we have to tell ourselves the dreaded word, "NO."

We all have goals, dreams and expectations. Yet years down the road we find ourselves in the same place we were when we first set the goal, or nowhere near where we had hoped to be. The reason for this is usually quite simple: we have made other things in our life more important than our goals, purpose and dreams.

We had the best intentions of living our life to the fullest, but the hustle and bustle of everyday life has a way of stealing our time and sucking all our energy leaving nothing left for the things that truly matter.

Your Turn

Speaking of the things that matter most, there is a very important question we must address before we go on. What are the top five things you want to accomplish in your lifetime?

It could include retiring at a specific age or with a certain amount in your bank account. Maybe it is writing a book, running a marathon, starting your own company, traveling to a certain destination, losing a specific amount of weight or patenting your invention. I am not asking about your Five Non-Negotiables, these are just five goals you want to accomplish.

1.

2.

3.

4.

5.

Now keeping in mind the five goals you just wrote down, ask yourself this: If you were to continue with the schedule, priorities and habits that you *currently hold* in your life, would you have reached the five goals you mentioned above within your lifetime? If you keep spending your money, time, focus and energy the way you are spending it, would you reach these five goals at the end of your life? Write your answer here.

It's Time For Neglect

If you have to answer no, perhaps it is time for some neglect in your life. When I asked myself the same question it was a real eye opener for me. I knew that I had goals that I wanted to accomplish, but I wasn't living my life in a way that would enable me to accomplish them. I guess I was just hoping that one day it would magically all work out and somehow I would accomplish them. Desire is not enough to reach our goals, we must also take action.

I kept telling myself, "one day" I would get started on my goals. The problem with "one day" was that it never seemed to come. Time kept flying by, but I wasn't making any progress. I realized that I was so busy running around wearing myself out trying to accomplish my to-do lists that I forgot about my goals and dreams and purpose. I forgot to make time for the most important things.

The point of the question is not to make you feel guilty. The point is to help you recognize where your life is headed if you don't STOP right now and apply change to your life. If you have been waiting for "one day" I am here to inform you that your "one day" is TODAY!

Let me say this another way: you literally have the power right now, this very minute to change the outcome of your life. If you will stop at this moment and determine that you are going to neglect the lesser things and make your goals top priorities you can and you will completely transform your life. The question is not CAN you change your future, the question is WILL you change your future?

The busyness of life can push our purpose and goals aside if we don't keep our hands on the wheel at all times. We can't live out our purpose unless we keep our lives pointed towards our goals and say "no" to some of the lesser things trying to steer us away.

Before we can even address the rest of our Five Non-Negotiables, we need to make room for them. Trying to stuff more into your life is not the answer. Like the pianist, if you want to be an expert at your goals and purpose you must neglect the things that do not contribute to your priorities. You must say no and simplify your life. When it comes to simplifying my life, I have consistently used two main methods: fasting and purging.

Fasting

Most people associate fasting with taking a break from food. While food fasts can be wonderful, fasting is not reserved to food alone. You can fast from anything: TV, social media, shopping. The purpose of the fast is to take a break from something to make room for other things.

Our lives can become too stuffed. Even if we want to shift the focus of our lives to our most important priorities, we are usually already too packed with insane schedules that we don't have enough energy, time or capacity to add in our goals and purpose. Let's not be held back from the greater things because we are too busy doing the lesser things. It's time to let go and make room for new things.

While trying to live out the Five Non-Negotiables, I set goals for my health. Unfortunately, I had an addiction to sugar for years. I was doing really good about eating healthy food, but I kept slipping up when it came to sugar. I would eat healthy all day and then at some point each day I would give in to my sugar cravings. Once I had one taste of sugar, there was no stopping me. I would end up eating the entire pint of ice cream in one sitting and set myself back in my goals another day.

This went on for years and then it dawned on me that I needed to take a complete break from sugar, cold turkey. This meant committing to a fast from sugar. If I could give my body a break from sugar and stop feeding the cravings, then it could have time to reset and help me stop craving sugar so strongly.

So I took a ninety day break from sugar (definitely some of the longest ninety days of my life). The first few weeks were so hard. I craved sugar constantly (especially after I ate anything salty), but I stayed committed and made it all ninety days. That one fast has changed my diet radically.

Since then, I have had much more control over sugar. It was as if sugar had a grip on me, but after the fast I got a grip over sugar. Now I can eat sugar occasionally, but I don't need it several times a day every day. I go most days without a single sugary treat at all. I reserve those for special occasions and splurges.

Even the times I get in a rut and find myself eating too much sugar again, it is a lot easier for me to get back on track than it was before I did the fast.

I don't think I could have gained control over my sugar cravings without a fast. I tried portion control and for some reason that wasn't enough. I literally needed to break free from sugar for a while to reset my body. Fasting allows us to do just that, reset ourselves and create space for something new.

If you don't have financial freedom, but you keep spending money on shopping sprees, perhaps it is time to take a fast from shopping. If you don't have enough time to work on your goals, but you spend two hours each night watching your favorite TV shows then perhaps it is time to take a little fast from television and give yourself those two hours to focus on your goals.

The nice thing about a fast is that it is only for a predetermined period of time. You only have to make it to a certain date, so there is light at the end of the tunnel to give you hope, it doesn't feel as endless and impossible as stopping forever.

Although I will say that most often when I do a fast, I never seem to go back completely to the way I was before. I enjoy the extra energy I get from eating healthier or I end up getting hooked on the book I am reading at night and actually enjoy reading more than watching TV.

Your Turn

Before we go any further, I want you to consider a fast. We are about to dive into the rest of the Five Non-Negotiables and you are going to need time and energy to focus on them. You will not have the ability to add in the necessary life changes to fulfill your goals and purpose in these areas of your life if it is already overstuffed.

Take a minute to evaluate your schedule and take an inventory of your time. Are there time wasters throughout your day that you could take a fast from while you are reprioritizing your life? Are there some foods or addictions that you need to fast from, or perhaps some impulse purchases or time scrolling through social media that you could take a break from to make room for some of the new habits we are about to make?

To help you get started, I have created a short list of common time-stealers. This is in no way a comprehensive list, just a few ideas to get you started.

Common Time-Stealers:

- Scrolling through social media

- Perusing the Internet

- Talking on the phone

- Watching TV

- Not delegating tasks or asking for help

- Volunteering for too many things

- Shopping

- Being a perfectionist

- Worrying

- Being unorganized

Keeping these things in mind, I have created some space below for you to write down one thing that you will commit to fast from during the journey through this book. Please take a minute to jot down your fasting goals and the amount of time you are committing to fast. It is okay to start slow, don't feel pressure to do too much.

I commit to fast from:

The amount of time I commit to fast is:

The reason I am committing to fast from this is...

Purging

Purging is another great way to simplify your life and make room for more important things. The difference between fasting and purging is that fasting includes taking a break while purging means completely getting rid of something.

There are some habits that are harmful and we need to purge them out of our lives completely. If you are a smoker and one of your goals is to become healthier then you are going to need to purge the habit of smoking from your life. You don't need to take a "fast" from smoking, you need to completely rid yourself of smoking or you will never be as healthy as you want to be.

Purging can be life changing. Letting go of things that are holding you back whether it is a bad habit, negative people, clutter, or limiting mindsets. There are many areas of our lives that we can purge to make room for something better.

Just as we did with fasting, I would like you to stop and take a minute to reflect on your life and consider if there is anything that you need to purge. Maybe it is using a credit card irresponsibly and racking up debt. It could be negative people who continue to drag you down or take advantage of you, or possibly things that you are reading or watching that are having a negative effect on your life.

Purging can also include setting boundaries. It doesn't necessarily always have to be completely eliminating something entirely from your life. For example, you can decide that you are going to purge watching daytime soap operas, but that doesn't mean that you have to purge all TV from your life.

You can set a boundary that you will not watch TV until 7pm at night to prevent yourself from binging on TV for the entire day. You can purge daytime TV, but that doesn't mean you still can't watch at night.

Sometimes when we are giving our best to make huge strides in life towards our goals and purpose, we end up like a swimmer with a rope tied to our ankle. We are trying to swim to the top and every time we make progress someone comes and tugs on the rope and yanks us back down to where we started. It might be time to bring out the scissors and cut the rope and set yourself free. What keeps pulling you under time and time again? Let's purge it once and for all.

Your Turn

Below is a list of ideas to get you started, but do not feel obligated to purge any of these. You need to purge what is right for you, so take the time to think it through. Also, you need to decide if this item is a complete purge from your life forever or if it is a purge with boundaries. Below is a short list of ideas just to get you thinking about what you might want to purge.

Ideas For Purging:

- Negative people
- Clutter in your home
- Credit cards
- Specific shows or media that are having a negative influence or effect on your life
- A bad eating habit
- Gossip (social media gossip counts too)
- Alcohol or substance use
- The words, "I can't" or "It's too hard" from your vocabulary
- Negative words and thoughts

I have created some space below for you to write down one thing that you would like to commit to purge from. The reason I only want you to purge one thing even if you have more than one in your mind is so we can start small. Just committing to fasting and purging is a huge leap towards your goals, but we don't want this to become too overwhelming.

Baby steps is the pace we are working at right now so if you are an overachiever and feel the need to purge it all right now, get over it. Take it slow and start with one thing and overachieve at fasting or purging at that one thing and then you can move on to the next item on your list.

Please take a minute to jot down the specific thing that you are ready to commit to purging out of your life. If you feel that it is too much to both fast and purge at the same time, feel free to choose one or the other. This is your journey, your book, your life. Go at your own pace, all I ask is that you don't quit and just keep putting one foot in front of the other.

I commit to purge from:

The reason why I am purging this from my life is…

Now take a minute to pull out your phone again (I know this is the best book ever because I keep giving you permission to use your phone). Add into your notes or wherever you keep your goals the list of what you are fasting or purging from and add in your whys.

When your alarm goes off in the morning this will be one of the goals you review to keep you on track. Write, "I'm letting go of things that are weighing me down" in the space below once you have added them into your phone.

After going through fasting and purging several times now, I actually get excited when it's time for me to purge. It is like a little mental, emotional, physical and spiritual spring cleaning. I feel so free once I do it.

Every time it gets hard during your fasting and purging process just keep reminding yourself why you are doing this: to make room for something better. Every day that you choose to stick to your fasting and purging you are getting closer to achieving your dream and living your purpose. You are on your way! You are no longer stuck in that rut, you are making real tangible progress in those areas of your life and that is exciting.

One Final Thing About Purging And Fasting

I love it when a great singer takes a song and turns it into what they call a "stripped down" version. A stripped down song means they have reduced the song to only the essentials. A song that might have included drums, a bass guitar and backup vocals now only includes a single acoustic guitar and the singer's raw voice.

This bare-bones version of the song is more intimate and reaches into your heart in a completely different way than the upbeat busier version. While I might like both versions I tend to be drawn to the simpler version because I am able to really focus on the message and purpose of the song. This simplistic version allows me to hear the same song in a new way. With all the instruments playing and the backup singers it is easy to drown out the authentic voice of the artist. In a stripped down version, the singer's voice is pretty much all they have.

It's time we strip some things down from your life and bring you back to the essentials, back to the authentic you again. Not the over-commercialized, stressed out, busy, tired and overwhelmed you, but instead the bare and stripped down version that is simple, authentic and pure.

Not who you feel the world is pressuring you to be, but who God created you to be. You are a gift to this world. Your life is a beautiful song meant to be heard and seen and enjoyed by the world. You were created for a reason. You have something extremely valuable to contribute to all of us. Your song is important and unique.

Don't let the noise of the world drown out your voice, your message and your joy. As we begin to strip away the noise the real you will emerge and the real you can begin the journey of taking steps to develop new habits to reach your goals. The world needs the authentic version of you, but first we must strip away all the noise so your voice can be heard.

Non-Negotiable #2

Health

10

Non-Negotiable #2: Health

"It is health that is real wealth and not pieces of gold and silver."
                                                                    -Gandhi

Why Does Our Health Really Matter?

You can have all the money and opportunity in the world, but if you don't have health then you have nothing. Without a healthy body and mind, we can't accomplish much.

Constantly feeling tired and having a foggy brain affects your ability to live with passion and motivation. Even something as small as allergies can affect our energy levels and ability to focus. Bloating and digestive issues can be miserable. When your health isn't good, everyday tasks can seem daunting and even the simple items on your to-do list can become a challenge.

Some of our freedom can even be taken away. We might become limited in the activities we can do, the types of jobs we can perform or the type of schedule we can maintain.

Do you realize that without your health, life really is no life at all? Now I know there are many people who have lived with and overcome huge health obstacles in their life and still done amazing things. Those people's lives and stories inspire me constantly, but I am not talking about those situations. I am talking about YOU. You neglecting your health. You putting excuses ahead of your health.

If you are reading this and you recognize that your health has not been a priority in your life then this is your literal wake up call. Now is the time to start taking better care of yourself.

Don't wait until you have a major health incident to finally take your health seriously. You have one life and one body. No matter how much money you have, you cannot buy a new body. If you don't take care of the one you have, you cannot get another.

You don't want to wake up one day and realize that it wasn't your body that let you down, it was your bad habits. You let your body down by your choices, all the little negotiations you made along the way.

The Time For Excuses Is Over

We have a huge list of reasons why we just can't workout or keep our cravings under control. The truth is these are lies that we tell ourselves to give us permission to not prioritize our health without having to feel guilty about it.

The time for excuses is over. Your life is far too valuable to not prioritize your health. So let's look at some of these lies disguised as excuses.

I Am Too Busy

Most of us know that we should be taking better care of ourselves, but in the midst of the busyness of life we don't make time for our health.

The problem is whether you feel like you have the time or not, neglecting your health will have negative consequences in your life. There is no way to get around neglecting your body and your body is not an area of your life that you want to take a shortcut in. You will end up paying big time later.

We all have the same 24 hours each day and we all decide how we are going to spend them. I understand that some people don't have as much time to exercise as others, but you don't have to become a gym rat to stay healthy.

You also don't have to go from never working out at all to going to the gym two hours a day. You can start small, start with a few days a week and as you progress you can start scheduling more workouts.

It doesn't have to be a long time, nor does it have to be overwhelming. The most important thing is to stop making excuses about not having the time and start making the time.

Taking Our Health For Granted

Even as an adult, some of the invincible child-like superhero beliefs seem to stay alive inside of us. We hear stories of others who have had heart attacks or high cholesterol, but for some reason we think we are immune to this sort of thing. We think we are invincible.

We believe that we will be young forever and that our bodies will never betray us. Unfortunately that is not the truth. When it comes to our body, we get out of it what we put into it. We need to stop abusing and neglecting our body.

It's Just My Genetics

While genetics can play a role in our health, it is still our personal responsibility to do the very best we can with the bodies we have been given. Having a genetic disease or ailment is not an excuse to throw in the towel.

You still have the personal responsibility to care for your body. You can't give up before you even get started because someone told you that you can't be healthy because of your genes. This is a wrong mindset that often strips away the motivation and drive to be physically healthy.

I Will Start Tomorrow

The famous last words, "I will start tomorrow," yet tomorrow never seems to come.

Stop procrastinating. Start today, start right now. Telling ourselves that we will start tomorrow is really another lie that we say to help us not feel so bad about procrastinating today.

You are worth it. Your life's purpose is worth it. We need you to show up today and be your best, so don't put your health off until tomorrow.

Your Turn

What are your top two excuses for not taking care of your health?

1.

2.

Write an argument against both of those excuses. For example, if your friend came to you and gave those same excuses for not being healthy and you knew that their future depended on them taking care of their body and if you knew they would be happier and healthier if they took care of themselves, what would you say to them to help them overcome the excuses?

What are these excuses stealing from you? A clear mind, a confident body, the energy you need to be as productive as your life needs you to be? Fun trips to the pool with friends or cute outfits at the store? What are these excuses taking from you right now?

Is hanging on to these excuses worth what they are costing you? Have you made a good deal with yourself when it comes to your health?

Hippocrates Wisdom

Hippocrates said it best, "Before you heal someone, ask him if he's willing to give up the things that make him sick."

Are you willing to give up the excuses and actually start doing the hard and necessary work of making your health a priority?

Unfortunately, there is no magic formula or easy way out. Health comes from consistent daily disciplines in our diet and exercise, yet excuse after excuse we continue to make for ourselves. I have one question for you... How are those excuses working out for you?

Are you healthy? If not then, STOP RIGHT NOW... it's time to make a change. There are two areas of health that are extremely important. How much you exercise and what you eat. Let's talk about both of these.

Exercise

I am not writing this section on exercise to be your trainer and tell you when to exercise and what types of exercises to do. There are many great resources and trainers out there for that. I am writing this to encourage you to actually make exercise a priority in your life. To make your health non-negotiable.

What Is Your Goal?

I hope that you are going to make a commitment to start exercising. I am not asking you to start training two hours a day, I am simply asking you to start exercising consistently if you aren't doing so.

You can start with baby steps, maybe ten minutes a day or only three days a week. Whatever you think you can commit to consistently.

I want you to set a realistic goal so that you can start being consistent, then once you have your first exercise goal down you can build on it.

Before you just jump into a new routine, let's make a plan to help you succeed.

Your Turn

What is your main fitness goal: lose weight, have more energy, increase your flexibility, stay healthy or ward off disease? Use the space below to write out your main fitness goal. Remember to make your goal specific, measurable and realistic. Only make one goal right now, we need to start with baby steps.

Here is where you are going to write out your "why." Why do you want to accomplish this goal? Use as many details as possible, because your why is your motivation.

Now add your fitness goal and your why into your phone with your other goals. When your alarm goes off to review your goals you will have it handy.

Once you have added your goal and why to your phone write "I am getting my butt in shape" below.

Your Needs

Now that you know what your goal is, let's talk about what you need to reach your goal.

You must assess your needs before you commit to jumping into a new workout regimen because if it doesn't meet your essential needs, you will eventually end up quitting. The exercise you choose needs to meet your: time schedule, childcare needs, ability levels, help achieve your fitness goals and be sustainable long term.

Personally some of my requirements include needing a gym that is close to my house. I know myself, if my gym is too far away then I will never go. I also must be able to go in the morning directly after dropping my kids off at school. I have tried joining workout classes that were in the middle of the afternoon and I just never seemed to be able to make it. I ended up being so inconsistent that it wasn't helping me at all.

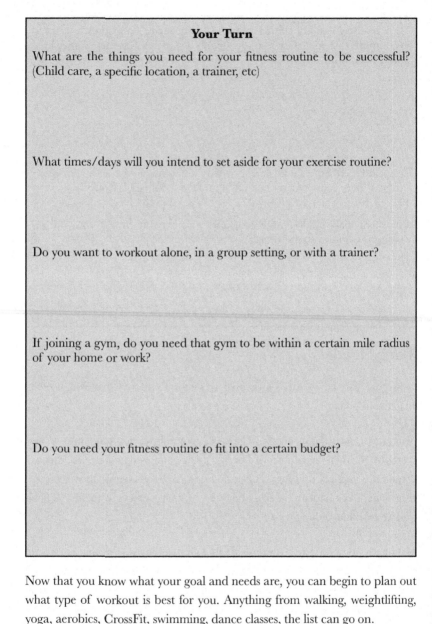

Your Turn

What are the things you need for your fitness routine to be successful? (Child care, a specific location, a trainer, etc)

What times/days will you intend to set aside for your exercise routine?

Do you want to workout alone, in a group setting, or with a trainer?

If joining a gym, do you need that gym to be within a certain mile radius of your home or work?

Do you need your fitness routine to fit into a certain budget?

Now that you know what your goal and needs are, you can begin to plan out what type of workout is best for you. Anything from walking, weightlifting, yoga, aerobics, CrossFit, swimming, dance classes, the list can go on.

You don't have to join a gym either, you can start a walking group with your neighbors or do Pilates online in your living room. Just be sure that your exercise routine is the right type of exercise for your health goals. If you want to run a marathon, don't join the body building gym.

Your Turn

What fitness routines or gyms meet both your goals and needs that you would like to consider trying? List them out below. If you aren't sure, do some research.

What is the first thing you are going to do to get started? Go to the gym and take a trial class? Call your friends and invite them to join your walking group? Whatever the first step is, write it down below.

What day/time are you going to take this first step?

Pull out your calendar and schedule it right now. Write, "Dear fat, prepare to die... sincerely, ME" below once you have completed this step.

I know all these detailed questions and steps might seem a little over the top (especially if you are not a detailed person), but the more detailed you are in the plan the better chance you have to achieve it and I so desperately want you to achieve your goals. So please be patient with me. I promise if you answer all the questions and make a plan you will be so far ahead of others in your ability to succeed at your goals.

Diet

When it comes to our diet, we seem to have negotiated ourselves into another bad deal. We trade the time and effort of preparing healthy meals for convenience. We know we should feed ourselves better, but what we don't realize is that this convenience comes at a huge cost.

Here are some recent stats about the health of Americans:

- Half of U.S. adults have diabetes or prediabetes.
- ⅔ of U.S. adults and ⅕ of children are overweight or obese.
- Poor nutrition is the #1 cause of illness in the United States and is responsible for more than half a million deaths per year.[1]

Americans are getting sicker. Chronic diseases and obesity are at an all time high. If you were to ask the average American how their body is feeling, most would have some sort of ailment they are struggling with.

Reasons For Our Bad Eating Habits

Most of what we eat is a habit. We tend to walk the same aisles in the grocery store every week and fill our baskets with the same items. We eat at the same times each day and have the same cravings.

We even eat at the same restaurants and order the same menu items. Our health is based on this pattern. Once we have created an unhealthy food habit, it can become so familiar to us that we don't realize the negative effect it is having on our health.

Let's take a minute to talk about some of these negative habits.

Convenience Eating

We pack our schedules so full that we are racing around from thing to thing all day long and we neglect to schedule in time to grocery shop and prepare healthy food. That is when convenience food comes into play.

Convenience food is one of the biggest traps I fall into. I get busy or I run myself so ragged that I am just too tired to cook a healthy dinner so I end up grabbing some quick frozen item for the family. In the words of John Wooden, "Failing to prepare is preparing to fail." Almost every time I have not planned ahead and prepared I have made a bad food choice.

There is nothing wrong with grabbing some quick and easy convenience food at the grocery store or local restaurant, but making convenience food your constant go-to at every meal isn't going to be your healthiest choice.

Emotional Eating

For many people food is almost like a drug. When we get stressed, depressed or bored we need our "fix" of food to make us feel better. Food gives us instant gratification almost like a literal high and for some reason it seems to make everything better while we are eating it. But as soon as the carton of ice cream is gone or the bag of chips is empty, we go from a sense of elation to guilt and sometimes even self-hatred.

Food was never meant to be an emotional void filler in our lives. Food serves the purpose of fueling our bodies and providing them with the proper nutrients to thrive and grow. When we see food as filling needs other than our source of nutrition, we can easily get caught up in unhealthy eating habits.

Overeating

Do you find yourself eating way more food than you should at each meal? Feeling like you have to finish everything on your plate whether you are hungry or not?

The Five Non-Negotiables

In America we have enormous portion sizes packed with fats, sugars and empty calories. Eating everything on our plate can sometimes mean consuming more calories in that one meal than we need for an entire day.

It is so easy to overeat especially when eating out or when eating straight out of the package or in my case the ice cream carton. It can be hard to know when to stop because it tastes so good.

Earned Eating

When life has been extra stressful we can tell ourselves, I am working hard so I deserve these treats. It is easy to completely sabotage our health goals by having a great workout and then telling ourselves that we have now earned a meal that is three times the amount of calories we just burned off.

You do need to have some balance though, you need to treat yourself sometimes, but we can definitely give ourselves "earned" treats much more than we realize.

Mindless Eating

It is so easy to grab a bag of chips while we are watching TV and not even realize we're eating. I have made myself a meal and sat down to eat it while scrolling through social media and once I finished eating I didn't even remember actually eating the food.

It was all gone and I never enjoyed a single bite because I was so consumed with my phone. When this happens I stare at my empty bowl still feeling hungry and wanting to eat more. Not paying attention to what you are eating and taking the time to enjoy the calories can leave you unsatisfied after a meal and craving even more food.

Famished Eating

If you wait until you are extremely hungry to decide what you are going to eat, the chances are you are going to grab the quickest thing you can find.

104

Any goals of eating healthy go flying out the window as your hunger pains and quickly fading blood sugar levels are screaming at you for food NOW!

When I get hungry I get hangry, you know the hungry/angry combination. When I am starving, I stop caring about my health because my stomach and emotions are screaming at me.

When you are hungry it is so easy to reach for that quick fix. That first scoop of ice cream is like heaven on my tongue. It is almost an out of body experience. With ice cream in hand I can take on the world. It is like a high, everything is right in the universe when I am eating Mint Chocolate Chip Ice Cream until thirty minutes later when the bloating starts and with the bloating comes the guilt.

With guilt comes more eating and with more eating comes gas. Oh yes I just went there. Full on flagellation fest and let me tell you everyone wants to clear the room.

Your Turn

We just covered several bad habits when it comes to eating. Take a minute and write down which of these habits you relate to most and why. Treat this almost as a journal entry and take your time with it. I want you to dig deep and think about the struggle.

Which two of these habits can you relate to most?

Why do you think these habits are your greatest struggle?

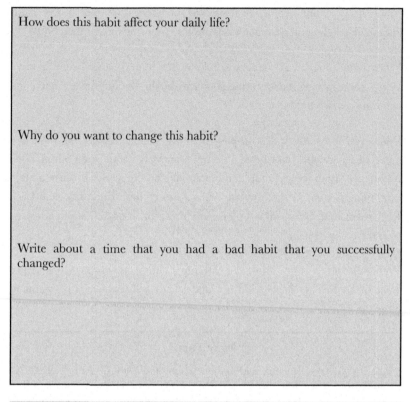

How does this habit affect your daily life?

Why do you want to change this habit?

Write about a time that you had a bad habit that you successfully changed?

Changing To Healthy Habits

Since most of what we eat is habitual, if we can switch just a few of our bad habits over to good ones, it can have a huge impact on our health.

Just the act of switching our breakfast to something healthier can lower our cholesterol levels, give us increased energy and less bloating throughout the day.

Changing a habit at the beginning can be difficult, but if you stick with it, there will come a point where your new healthy eating routine has become a new habit and with almost as little effort as your unhealthy diet took, you can maintain your new healthier habit. I know that sounds crazy, but I promise you it is true.

You have to get through the beginning though and not quit just because it's hard. It will get easier the longer you make healthy choices. Also, as you begin to see the results in your body like feeling better, having more energy and losing weight, you will become even more motivated to keep the new healthy eating habits going.

Let's explore some ideas on baby steps we can take to begin getting healthier.

How To Make Better Food Choices

Start With One Thing

When I started trying to eat healthier I had limited experience cooking healthy items, but I was determined to learn how to make tasty vegetables. To make it simple I started with just one vegetable, asparagus.

I started by reading about different ways to cook asparagus and I watched some videos with asparagus recipes online. Then I went to the store and bought asparagus and started practicing.

Only focusing on one vegetable made the task simple enough that I could manage it. If I tried to roast the vegetable and the family didn't like it, I could go back to the recipes and try another way the next night until I found a way that most of the family liked that vegetable.

Once I got the hang of asparagus I moved on to broccoli and then brussels sprouts. It seemed slow in the beginning, but within a few months I had several vegetables that I could cook pretty decently and quickly. My family was already eating more vegetables.

The way you cook a vegetable can dramatically change its flavor and texture. If you tried a vegetable and didn't like it, try cooking it another way. You just might be surprised at how much you like a vegetable if it is cooked differently.

Take baby steps so you don't get overwhelmed. Be smart and cut the big problem down into bite sized pieces that are manageable to you. You can do this.

Your Turn

What is the one vegetable or recipe or small step that you are going to start with?

Learn To Meal Prep

Dream with me for a minute. Imagine it is Monday morning, you get out of bed and the following is already done:

- Most of the grocery shopping is done for the entire week.
- Dinners are already made for the next few nights.
- The dinner dishes are already washed because the cooking was done ahead of time.
- The food is all washed, cut and prepped for the dinners you will cook later in the week.
- Your breakfasts, lunches and snacks for most of the week are done.

How would that make you feel? Amazing, I know!

When you take the time to meal prep that is exactly how you get to start your week. I cannot tell you how nice it is to have the majority of the shopping and cooking and dishes already done before my week even starts!

Schedule time each week to go grocery shopping and prepare healthy meals. This can seem overwhelming at first, but once you get into the new routine, it actually ends up saving you a lot of time and money.

I usually plan out my meals and do my grocery shopping on Sunday. I also do my big cooking and any food preparations that I can do ahead of time like chopping, washing and marinating on Sundays.

Then on Wednesdays or Thursdays I run to the grocery store and pick up any other ingredients I might need and throw together my next set of meals for the rest of the week. I only spend about two nights per week with the major cooking. The rest of the week is either more simple meals that don't take a whole lot of cooking or eating the meals I already prepped.

So I sacrifice a few hours twice a week and then I don't have to think about cooking, a messy kitchen full of pots and pans or grocery shopping for the rest of the week.

Another great thing about meal prepping is that you can pre-portion all your food in storage containers which can help you control portion sizes. Meal prepping also takes out the decision making when you are too tired or busy to cook healthy food.

There is no stress over figuring out what to eat. Your meal is already made and in the fridge waiting for you. Once you find a routine that works for you, you will begin to love having your food already made and planned out for you most of the week.

Your Turn

Get out your calendar and schedule in a time that you are going to do some meal prepping this week. Write "Prep once, eat healthy all week", below once you have it scheduled.

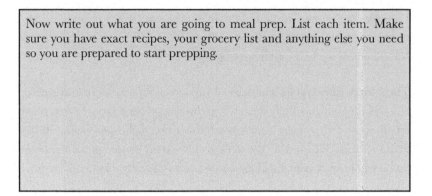

Now write out what you are going to meal prep. List each item. Make sure you have exact recipes, your grocery list and anything else you need so you are prepared to start prepping.

Be Prepared For Eating Out

When eating out at a restaurant that is not one of your usual spots, look at the menu ahead of time. Most restaurants have a website where you can view their menu and many even have their nutritional information online. You can decide what you are going to eat before you get there.

This can take a lot of stress off trying to make a healthy choice in the spur of the moment. Since you already made up your mind before you arrived at the restaurant you will have less chance of being swayed by all the fancy photos of the unhealthy food strategically scattered all over the menu.

Your Turn

Make a list of the top five restaurants that you eat at the most often. It can be fast food or regular sit down restaurants.

1.

2.

3.

4.

5.

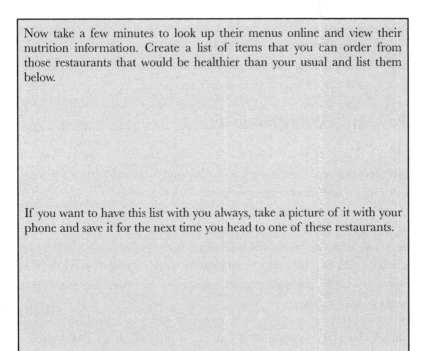

Now take a few minutes to look up their menus online and view their nutrition information. Create a list of items that you can order from those restaurants that would be healthier than your usual and list them below.

If you want to have this list with you always, take a picture of it with your phone and save it for the next time you head to one of these restaurants.

Portion Control

One of the number one ways to overeat is to eat food directly out of the container you bought it in. Eating the chips straight out of the bag is almost a sure way to end up eating the entire bag in one sitting. When you want to snack, take the time to calculate the portion you want to eat and put it in a separate bowl and eat it from there. This will help you to control your portion sizes.

Don't Buy Unhealthy Foods

If you buy it and put it in your pantry then you will end up eating it at some point. So if a food doesn't meet your health goals, then just don't buy it. If it isn't in the pantry then it won't be possible to eat it at midnight when you are craving a snack.

Like everything in life you need balance. I am not encouraging some extreme diet. It's OK to splurge and eat unhealthy foods sometimes. I am simply hoping to help motivate you to make healthier choices in a balanced way. To take care of your body, you only get one.

Pay Now Or Pay Later

My grandma Jane always used to tell me when it comes to health, "You will pay now with your time and money to buy and prepare healthy food or you will pay later with doctor bills and medical appointments."

Let's stop making all these little negotiations with our diets that are adding up to big consequences we will have to pay for later. You know that it is time to stop negotiating with your health. Earlier you set a goal to start exercising and we created a game plan to get you started. Now we are going to set a goal for what you eat.

You can set a goal to drink more water or stop eating after 8 PM. Choose a small goal that is realistic. When I was addicted to sugar I used to eat a pint of ice cream every night. This had become such a habit that I still needed something cold to eat at night. So I bought these huge grapefruits and put them in the fridge so they were cold and I bought those special grapefruit spoons so I could feel like I was scooping it out of a bowl. I started eating cold grapefruit with a spoon instead.

It wasn't the same as ice cream, but it allowed me to still eat something cold for months until I finally just completely weaned off the habit of eating that late at night. I changed that habit in baby steps.

Start really small if you have to, but get started on making your health a priority. If you feel like you have already committed to exercising in this chapter and tackling food as well is too much that is ok. You can focus on one at a time if you need. Just commit to one and be sure it is non-negotiable.

Your Turn

What is your non-negotiable goal when it comes to your health? Is it food related or exercise related or both? Write your non-negotiable goal below.

Now write out your why. This is your motivation so make sure it is a very strong why. Give as much detail as possible.

Put this goal and your why into your phone or wherever else you put all your other goals to review each day. Write, "I am proud of myself for making my health a priority again" below once you have completed this task.

Get out your calendar and schedule in your new goal. Exactly what time and day/s you will be taking action towards your goal. Write "I can't wait to feel good and look good as I get healthier" below once you have scheduled it in.

11

Get Off The Hamster Wheel

"The hamster called. He wants his home back."

-James Patterson

We have all been to the pet store and seen those cute furry little rodents running as fast as their tiny legs will take them on the stationary wheel in their cage. They are running so hard, but they are getting nowhere. As much as we don't like to admit it, we can probably relate in some ways to the hamster.

> *Hamster Wheel: A monotonous, repetitive, unfulfilling activity, especially one in which no progress is achieved.*[1]

Why are we running low on time, money and energy to live out our purpose? Because we are spending much of our lives running on a hamster wheel. We are running as fast and hard as we can, but we are making little progress because we are spending some of our resources on monotonous, repetitive and unfulfilling activities in which no progress is achieved. This reminds me of the definition of insanity.

> *Insanity: To keep doing the same thing over and over and expecting different results.*

Life can feel like one big insane hamster wheel. We are running around exhausting ourselves and all the while getting nowhere. We are so busy chasing after money, success, affirmation and attention or we are running from fear, insecurities and pain.

We think that we will find what we really want or need if we can just keep running, but the problem isn't that you aren't running fast enough, it is that you are running on a freaking hamster wheel! Which means you are chasing empty or lesser things hoping to catch what you really want.

As ridiculous as running on a hamster wheel can sound, it is actually a lot easier to get caught on a hamster wheel than you think. One of the greatest dangers of the hamster wheel is that it keeps us too busy, busy doing nothing. This busyness steals the time and energy we need to slow down and reevaluate our lives. If we don't jump off the hamster wheel and slow down then we will not recognize where we are going wrong.

Unfortunately, parts of my life are a great example of this. I am a perfectionist by nature and I set impossible expectations on myself all the time. One of the biggest ways I have done this to myself is in the area of motherhood.

When my first child was born I had so many crazy expectations about what makes a good mother. I had no real experience of my own so I basically took all the women who I thought were practically perfect in their area of expertise and decided I would have to be just like them in every way. I didn't only expect myself to be as good as they were in their area of expertise, I expected myself to be as good as every woman I knew in every area of their expertise.

One of these areas was baby food. I built up this idea in my mind when my first daughter was born that in order to be a good mom I had to:

- Grow all my own organic food.
- Make all my own baby food only from the items I grow in my organic garden.
- Only feed my baby the food I make myself.
- Failure to do this equals failure as a mother.

I had heard and seen other women who had amazing gardens and their entire family only ate the food they grew from their own land and I decided of course I must do the same or I am shortchanging my child.

This meant I had to grow this incredible organic garden that was big enough to fully nourish my child while living in an apartment so the only place I could grow anything was a small patio.

This is actually embarrassing to write and for those of you who have had children you are probably laughing your heads off right now knowing the realities of raising kids, but as a new mom these were the standards I put on myself. Basically I built this crazy hamster wheel idea that I was going to spend a lot of my time and energy chasing after each day believing that if I could run hard enough and fast enough to accomplish all these tasks then I would be a great mother.

While making your own baby food is a great thing, my entire focus was on doing everything perfect so I could be the perfect mother. I thought that if I could achieve being the perfect mother then I would truly be happy and my children would all turn out perfect. It wasn't about the food, it was about me being a perfect mom. Trying to keep up with all the other "perfect" moms out there who were growing their own organic baby food.

I didn't stop with the baby food though, there was also the expectation of always having a perfectly clean house, never having more than one load of dirty laundry at a time, dusting my blinds twice a week (each blind by hand individually…no duster here), giving my kids the perfect schedule even if it completely wore me out, the list can go on and on. I think I will stop here and save myself the humiliation. I know you guys think I am silly, but I am being serious here.

Each morning I would wake up and climb on that hamster wheel and run my little heart out. I would race around the house trying to make everything perfect. Every single time I tried to grow my own garden it would die or get eaten by bugs. Literally every time.

I would cry and beat myself up about not having a green thumb. When the house would get out of order I would look around feeling overwhelmed and teary eyed and start cleaning up again for the tenth time that day because if the house wasn't perfect then neither was I.

For seven years I tried so hard to grow the perfect garden and I literally had never produced anything from any garden except basil. We are talking NOTHING. For some reason I am great at growing basil though! That's my only claim to fame in the garden world. I can grow basil like it's nobody's business.

Every year my garden was a disaster with bugs or fungus or plants that just wouldn't produce anything. So then I would proceed to spend even more time and money buying organic bug killers and fungicides.

I would go outside every day to weed and water the plants. I would cut the dead leaves off and care for them. If you have ever grown a garden then you know just how much work they really are to keep up. Yet year after year my gardens were epic failures. It has now become a family joke that I have a brown thumb. If you want a plant to die just give it to Chelsea, everyone says.

Once we were finally able to buy a house with a large backyard I was determined things were going to turn around for me. I created my biggest garden ever and spent hundreds of dollars on it. Money that, honestly, we didn't have at the time, but my husband knew how much this meant to me so he went with it.

I was so excited to finally be the perfect mom with my own full garden. That year the same thing happened as all the years before, my garden was a disaster. Hardly anything grew and what did grow the bugs and birds quickly ate up before they were even ripe.

I spent more time on that garden than I had on any garden before it because of its size. I hand watered it each day and picked weeds and tended to every little need the garden might have and still no success. I spent even more money on kits to test the soil, organic bug sprays and fertilizers. Another epic failure.

Once again my lack of success made me feel like a failure. Then all of a sudden one day I had an epiphany: If I had spent a fraction of the money I had spent on the garden on buying organic produce I could have bought enough organic produce for my family for years. I was spending so much time, energy and money on this garden because I believed it would make me a "good" mother.

Instead of focusing on defining who I was authentically as a mother, discovering what kind of mother I really was supposed to be in my own way, I spent time and energy becoming the mother I thought I was supposed to be.

Where did these crazy ideas of motherhood come from? From comparison, looking at all the other mothers around me and using their images and their unique motherhood to define my own motherhood.

We look at our friend who always has their kids dressed like they just stepped out of a magazine and we think we need to be like that. Then we look at our friends with the perfectly clean house all the time and so we think we need to be just like her.

The next thing we know we have a huge list of expectations that we have put on ourselves due to comparing ourselves with others. This list then becomes the hamster wheel we run everyday.

The Five Non-Negotiables

Trying to be like everyone else will keep you on the hamster wheel your entire life. Saying no to the things that are not meant for you will give you freedom.

It is ok to not be good at everything. We need to be secure enough to say: this is who I am and this is who I'm not. I might not be a gardener, but I can run a fast mile. I am so bad with math that I can't even help my elementary kids with their homework, but I am great at coaching their soccer team.

There is only one you! No one else can replace you or do what you do the way you do it. You are unique, you are a gift to this world. Spend your time and energy discovering who your unique self is and put everything you've got into mastering the art of being yourself. Run towards your dreams, not in an endless circle.

Stop comparing yourself with others, jump off that hamster wheel and soar at being yourself! You will be amazed at how much farther you get in life by being yourself than you have in the past by trying to imitate others.

As Oscar Wilde said: "Be yourself; everyone else is already taken."

For me, part of getting off the hamster wheel was to stop growing my own garden.

Growing your own organic garden is a great thing, but it wasn't "my" thing. I realized I was toiling in vain, trying to prove to myself that I was a "perfect" mom. Stressing myself out, spending money we didn't have and time I shouldn't have spent on a garden.

I finally released myself from the mindset of "good moms grow their own organic gardens." I can't tell you how freeing that was. I can still be a great mother and not grow a garden. In fact I could be the worst gardener in the world and still be a good mom. I can buy good produce from the grocery store and the local farmer's market and it's just fine.

While I respect and look up to those who have their own gardens, I might even be a little envious of them, it is just not something I should be doing myself in this season of life.

We can't do it all, we weren't created to do it all. We say that we believe that we are each created as unique individuals with a unique purpose, but when it comes to our own lives, we aren't satisfied with only fulfilling our own unique purpose. We feel like we have to fulfill every purpose, do it all, be as good as others who are thriving in that area because it is part of their gift or purpose.

I look back now on all the stress and pressure I put on myself over this garden that was never even meant to be. I am tired of wasting time, energy and money on the wrong things, the lesser things.

Why did I think that having perfectly clean floors or all the beds in the house made without wrinkles was worth my sanity? Why did I believe that having everything organized and all my errands run by noon equaled fulfillment? I look back on that tired version of myself with pity. I was trying so hard to do everything right and I was missing out on what really mattered.

There is a saying that goes, "The way you gain something is the way you have to keep it." If I gain my self-worth and fulfillment in accomplishing tasks, then I am going to have to spend my entire life accomplishing more and more tasks in order to remain fulfilled.

If I have to be perfect to receive love, then I will have to spend my entire life trying to be perfect in order to feel loved. If I gain success by working myself to death and ignoring my health, then I am going to have to continue to work myself to death to maintain my success.

I wish I had been better focused on the things that mattered most in the first few years of my girl's lives. I missed out on so much true joy, peace and rest.

Your Turn

Jumping off the hamster wheel takes courage because we are so used to our daily run, that we are afraid if we don't jump back on the wheel tomorrow morning something bad might happen. We have this false sense of security that somehow by running on the hamster wheel we are holding everything together, all the while we are falling apart on the inside. The hamster wheel is a trap, a false sense of security and accomplishment. It is a lesser way of living and a shortchanging of who we really are. Enough is enough. I stopped growing a garden, what are you going to stop doing today? Write it below.

Do you have unrealistic expectations? Are you putting a ton of time and energy into something just to impress others or feel good about yourself, but it isn't really part of your purpose in this season? Are you putting undue pressure on yourself in certain areas of your life that really should be put on the back burner?

Take a minute to think through your daily schedule. Are there any activities that you now realize are hamster wheels in your life? Are there wrong mindsets and expectations that you are holding onto that are keeping you on a hamster wheel? Write about them below.

Now write out why you believe these activities and mindsets are hamster wheels in your life.

12

Mindset

"If you realized how powerful your thoughts are, you would never think a negative thought."

-Peace Pilgrim

The Power Of Your Mind

Our minds are incredibly powerful. When God created our minds he intended to give us a gift that was so powerful it could be used to shape our entire lives and affect everything about us, our words, actions and even our physical body down to the cellular level. Let me give you a few fascinating facts about our minds.

1. "Thoughts are real and physical things that take up mental real estate in the brain", according to Dr. Caroline Leaf, author of *Switch on Your Brain.*[1] They are not abstract things floating through

space. Thoughts change the physical structure of our brain. Scientists can see thoughts forming through the use of technology.

2. Scientists used to think that our brains were fixed, therefore the way we thought and behaved was set. We now know that our brains have the incredible ability to reprogram themselves and adapt. Our mind's ability to change the brain is called Neuroplasticity. Meaning our brains are malleable, they can change and regrow.

3. Your thoughts control all of your behavior: your actions, words and attitudes.

Our Thoughts Change Our DNA

We also know that making physical changes to our brains also makes physical changes to our bodies.

Did you know that your thoughts have the ability to change the shape of your DNA? There was an experiment done by The Institute of HeartMath which is a non-profit organization that helps people reduce stress.

In the experiment they tested the relationship between our DNA and our thoughts and feelings. After being trained in how to generate deep feelings, twenty eight trained researchers were given twenty eight vials of DNA.

When the researchers were thinking and feeling fear, anger, frustration and stress the DNA actually became shorter. It started to bind up. The DNA also responded by switching off some of the DNA codes. This showed the researchers physical evidence of how our thoughts affect us down to the cellular level.

When we think and feel stressed out, our DNA binds up. When we feel shut down by negative emotions, part of our body's DNA codes shut down too.

When the researchers switched their thinking and feeling to gratitude, love and appreciation the DNA became longer and the DNA codes switched back on again.[2]

It is not just our DNA that determines who and what we are. The environment that our DNA lives in plays a role in how our DNA is expressed, which in turn determines how our DNA shapes us.[3]

"After two decades of studies, HeartMath researchers say factors such as the appreciation and love we have for someone or the anger and anxiety we feel also influence and can alter the outcomes of each individual's DNA blueprint."[2]

Thoughts are real physical things, not just an invisible force in our minds. Our thoughts actually occupy mental real estate in our brain. Our brain's structure is always changing minute by minute as we think.

Your DNA alone does not determine who you become and what you are capable of, the environment that your DNA lives in determines which parts of your DNA will express themselves and which parts will be shut down.

To quote an article from The HuffPost titled, *How Your Thoughts Change Your Brain, Cells and Genes:*

> *"Your biology doesn't spell your destiny, and you aren't controlled by your genetic makeup. Instead, your genetic activity is largely determined by your thoughts, attitudes, and perceptions. … (this) places you in the driver's seat. By changing your thoughts, you can influence and shape your own genetic readout.*
>
> *You have a choice in determining what input your genes receive. The more positive the input, the more positive the output of your genes. … lifestyle choices can be directly traced to the genetic level and is proving the mind-body connection irrefutable. At the same time, research into epigenetics is also emphasizing how important positive mental self-care practices are because they directly impact our physical health."[4]*

The environment your DNA lives in is largely based on your thoughts.

Our thoughts physically affect our bodies.

The good news about this is that if our thoughts change our brains, and we have control over our thoughts, then we can change our brains which will change our lives.

Your Turn

What type of environment are you giving your DNA? Positive or negative?

Being Locked Out

I keep my car key and house key separate. I know I am strange like that, but that's just how I roll. I remember one time I left to run some errands while Michael stayed home with the girls. When I got home our front door was locked. I wasn't expecting it to be locked since Michael had said he was staying home.

Apparently, the girls had convinced Daddy that they needed to go out for ice cream, so they were out on a date. I was really frustrated because I was tired and I had groceries that needed to get into the refrigerator.

I tried calling him and he didn't answer which made me even more frustrated. I looked inside the window and I could see our puppies relaxing in the house wagging their tails staring back at me. They were so content enjoying the air conditioning while I was burning up in the sun. I didn't know what else to do so I just sat on the porch and pouted. Poor Chelsea, locked out of her own house.

About thirty minutes into my pouting Michael showed up and asked me what I was doing on the porch. I told him that I was locked out. He said to me, "When I left the house I looked to make sure you had your key before I locked the door." I told him that I didn't think I had my key because I didn't remember grabbing it.

He said, "Well your key wasn't where you usually hang it so I figured you brought it with you." I stopped and opened up my purse and looked inside and there was my house key. It was in my purse the entire time. I had been pouting on my front porch letting all my food spoil in the heat when I had the key with me the entire time.

How many times have we found ourselves sitting outside pouting on the porch looking inside the window at others enjoying the life that we want for ourselves when the truth is that we actually have the key to get inside with us all along? We long for more from life, but we settle for less.

We want meaningful relationships, but we don't reach out because we are afraid of being rejected. We want to try something new, but we are afraid of failure. We want to build a business, but we feel unqualified. So instead we stand outside on the front porch staring at our dreams, but never unlocking the door. We choose to be a prisoner, locked out of the life we want.

Our mind has become our prison instead of our key.

Self-Made Prisons

It is the self limiting beliefs in our minds that locks us out and creates these prisons. Each of us has a set of limiting beliefs.

- I will never get out of debt. It doesn't matter how hard I try, I'll never have financial freedom.
- I'm always going to be overweight, it's just the way I was born and there is nothing I can do about it.
- I am not good enough, no matter how hard I work or what I do to impress people it is never enough.
- I can't change. I have tried so many times before and I alway fail because I just don't have the willpower to stick with anything.

The Five Non-Negotiables

Most of the limitations we have in our lives are actually set by ourselves. Through our own minds. These beliefs are little cages that we have locked ourselves in. What you think and believe is what you will produce. Every one of your limiting beliefs are lies that are holding you captive.

Rather than face the truth, we allow ourselves to become deceived into thinking that our limitations are caused by some outside force:

- We don't have enough time.
- We have the wrong personality.
- We have made too many mistakes.

The truth is, all of those proposed "limitations" are not really limitations at all. They are excuses to stay the same. The only limitations are the prison walls we have placed our own selves in through our self limiting beliefs.

A lie that is believed to be true will affect your life as if it were true. Meaning what you believe, even if it is not true, will still shape your life according to that lie.

If you think you aren't good enough then your mind will begin to cause you to behave in a way that will make you fail. If you think you can never accomplish that task, your mind will shut down the parts of your brain that would help you accomplish that task.

I want you to recognize the power that you have to change your life through your mind. I want you to wake up and realize that you already have the keys to your freedom within you. You aren't locked out of the life you want because you don't have the keys to get in, you are locked out of the life you want because you aren't using the key you already have. Your mind is the cage you are trapped in, but your mind also holds the key to set you free.

Your Turn

What self-made prisons have you created in your mind? What lies do you believe today because of negative things said over you as a child or mistakes you have made or times you have tried and failed? Write some of these lies out here.

Our Mind Is The Key

Everything you ever say or do was first a thought. Your mind holds the key to your life. What you believe is what you will do and become. I sat outside in the heat locked out of my house because I believed that I didn't have my keys with me. I had the solution, but I didn't believe I did so I was locked out. The same goes for your life. You have the ability to do so much more than you are doing. The question is do you believe it?

Your mind is actually a gift from God. It makes me mad that our thinking has become so messed up that what was meant to be a tool to help us live a full life has become a prison. A place where we constantly replay our mistakes, beating ourselves up over every bad choice we have ever made. Where we judge others and ourselves unfairly.

Our minds have become a safe haven for our fear, pain and doubt to live unchallenged. Where voices repeatedly tell us we aren't good enough or that we are too fat or too ugly. A prison where the guilt is dripping off the walls and the anxiety and stress is choking us.

Imagine if your kids grew up in a home that was a match to the prison in your mind? Imagine if they grew up in all of that negativity and self hate and negative self-talk. Imagine if they grew up in a home with that much guilt and fear and shame and stress.

You would never put your kids in a home filled with such negativity, yet we let ourselves live in this home all day everyday. Your mind is a home for who you are on the inside. Your mind is where your beliefs and emotions come from.

If your mind is not a healthy home for your children to live in then it isn't healthy for you either. It's time to make a change. You deserve a healthy home. A safe place for your dreams, goals and self to live and rest in.

Your mind should not be a prison and if the words I just used to describe a prisoner's mind are ringing true with you then it is time to reset your mind. It is time to pull out the keys and get the heck out of that place.

Only you can set your mind free though, no one else can do it for you.

Lie Detector Test

All of the lies and excuses and chains we have put on our own lives through our thoughts need to stop. Stop just believing whatever comes into your mind, or whatever your feelings are telling you.

It's time to pull out the lie detector and call these lie's bluffs.

My family loves playing the card game B.S. (If you are not familiar with this card game, here are the rules.)

The game starts by dealing out every single card in the deck evenly among all the players. The first player to play must lay down an ace, then the second player must lay down a two and the third player must lay down a three and so on all the way to King. Once you have made it from Ace to King then you start at Ace again and keep going around and around in numerical order until someone wins by running out of the cards in their hand.

You lay the cards face down so that no one can see them, therefore you don't know for sure if someone is really laying down the card they are supposed to or if they are lying about it. When it is your turn and you don't have the specific card you are supposed to lay down, you have to put down a different card and lie about it and hope that no one calls you out on B.S.

For example, if it was my turn and we were on the number eight and I didn't have an eight in my hand then I would have to lay down a different card and lie and say that it was an eight.

Hopefully everyone believes me and we move on to the next person who would then need to lay down a nine. But if someone thinks I am lying then they will call B.S.

If they were right and they caught me in a lie then I would have to take the entire stack of cards, but if they were wrong and I really did lay down an eight, then they would have to be the one to take the entire set of cards.

Remember, the goal is to get rid of all your cards so you don't ever want to have to pick up the pile.

My husband is really good at B.S., it is so hard to tell if he is lying or if he really had that particular card. He keeps a straight face the entire game. He doesn't talk much, he just stares at his cards. It drives me crazy that I can't tell what he is thinking.

My cute little daughter Reese though, I can read her like a book. She tries so hard to fake us out, but we all know when she is lying. She has such a hard time faking us out that many times she will start laughing while she is laying the card down and we all know that means she is lying. If she doesn't laugh then she will smirk or blush. Poor girl never wins at B.S.

When it comes to our thought life, we need to get really good at B.S. When our thoughts are lying to us we need to be able to recognize them right away and call B.S. We need to tell those thoughts, "I am not accepting that, I am not believing that. I am not going to allow these lies to shape my life and put me in a made up prison."

The Five Non-Negotiables

Being a good lie detector can be tricky though because the lie will try its best to tell you it's an eight even if it really is a queen of hearts. If you aren't guarding your mind and being watchful of your thought life it can be really easy for lies to slip in right past you. Lies do their very best to disguise themselves as the truth.

You don't have to believe every thought that comes into your head just because you thought it. A lot of things that run through my head are no good and I have to constantly call B.S. on them and reject them. You can do the same thing.

Some of our lies are like Reese playing B.S.- easy to recognize. But other lies we have believed for so long that we don't even recognize them as B.S. anymore. In fact we believe them and base our lives on them.

We need to start taking inventory of our thoughts and put them through a lie detector test. We need to start thinking about what we are thinking about and sift out the lies and hang onto the truth.

The longer we believe something the harder it can be to recognize it for the lie that it is. It's time to dig deep and search diligently for the truth so that we can be set free.

If lies are the enemy that we need to combat, then the weapon of choice to defeat them must be the truth. My standard for truth is the Bible. If it doesn't line up with what God says about me, then I refuse to believe it. People's opinions and words about me are too fickle, constantly changing day by day. I want to build my life on something more steady than the words of people. Following God's truth has set me free in so many ways.

Your Turn

What is the standard of truth that you base your life on? How do you know what is the truth and what is a lie?

We Can Be Our Own Brain Surgeons

So what can we do to reprogram our brain and control our thought lives? How can we recognize the lies and keep them out?

When we start thinking about something new or we start thinking a different way about something, we are creating new thought networks in our brain. We are changing the physical structure of our brain.

To change our life we have to change our mind through changing our thoughts. Changing a negative thought like, "I can't do that" to a positive thought like, "I can do that" sets off a huge wave of neural activity in the brain as your brain begins to create a new neural pathway that enables you to begin to believe that you can actually do it.

As you continue to think positively day after day, the neural pathways that say, "you can do it" get stronger and stronger and the negative neural pathways that are now being neglected get smaller and smaller. The brain is similar to our muscles in that if you don't use it you will lose it.

So if you stop using negative thinking, you will start losing it.

God knew that we would need help with our minds so he created our brains in such a way that every morning when you wake up you have thousands of new baby nerve cells that are ready for you to use as you want?[5]

Meaning you can use them to think positive thoughts and reinforce and grow positive thinking or you can use them to think negatively. Maybe this is what the Bible means in Lamentations 3:23, when it says, "His mercies are new every morning."

The process of the formation of these baby nerve cells is called neurogenesis. You can use these baby nerve cells to start breaking down negative thought patterns in your life and building a new self image in your mind. We get new ones every morning, we need to use them wisely.

According to Dr Leaf, when we pull a thought out of our subconscious and into our conscious mind it becomes malleable and vulnerable. At this stage we are able to reshape it. We can use our new baby nerve cells to help us.

If you have a negative thought deep inside you that you strongly believe, for example, "I will never be in shape" and you want to change it, you need to bring that thought to your mind and then replace it with what you want to believe.

You could change your thought to, "I can become a healthy person by making healthy choices everyday." In that moment you are physically creating a new neural pathway in the brain. It is a new thought. It is weak and fragile, but you have given birth to that new thought and it is now taking up mental real estate in your brain.

As you refuse to think on the negative thoughts, the neurons connected to that negative thought will stop getting the signals they are used to and they will start to weaken and break apart. Eventually the emotion once attached to that negative thought will begin to fade and break apart as well.

If you have a positive thought that you start thinking about daily then the neurons will begin to fire towards that positive thought everyday creating a stronger bond with each passing day.

I want to pull a section from Dr. Caroline Leaf's book called, *Switch On Your Brain* because I want you to hear from a real professional exactly how thoughts take up actual space in your brain. In fact a lot of the research on mindset that I have discovered and included in this book is from her so I want to be sure to give her credit. In this section Dr. Leaf is explaining how a new thought takes physical shape in our mind as we think about it more and more until it becomes our new way of thinking.

> "In the brain, automatization physically looks like lots more tree branches that are thick and well established, with many branches interconnecting with other thought networks. And if you could zoom in closely to the connections the branches grow from, you would see little things called spines. These spines change shape, from a bump around 7 days, to a lollipop shape at around 14 days, to a mushroom shape around 21 days as the thought becomes stronger. This is because the proteins change progressively by day 21, with peak changes being at 7 and 14 days to become self-sustaining proteins which are long-term memory."

These bumps and mushrooms and lollipops are constantly growing and changing in our brains depending on our thoughts. To bring this complex concept down to my level: good thoughts will grow good mushrooms and negative thoughts will produce negative mushrooms.

The point I am trying to get across to you with all of this scientific brain jargon is that your thoughts are real tangible things and that you can physically change them in your brain through your thoughts. Your thoughts physically create these mushrooms and lollipops. You get to decide if they are good lollipops or bad ones.

The neuroplastic trait of the brain is incredible because it allows you to tweak and strengthen the good thoughts you want to have and remove the ones that are harming you. Usually neurons make connections with each other based on the strongest signals given out. The neurons that are used the most (the thoughts we think on most) give the greatest signal. Other similar neurons are then looking to connect with those neurons to create even stronger connections.[6]

Neurons with very little signal continue to fade over time as their connections get lost.

Sometimes who we really are has been overshadowed by who we have allowed ourselves to become through our thought lives. Through the lies we have accepted and the negative thoughts we have dwelled on.

Our genes lay dormant inside until we switch them on by sending them a signal through our thoughts. If our thoughts are negative then the full potential of our DNA will not be switched on. We have so much more potential in our genes, but our thoughts determine how much of that potential we switch on.

When you understand the power of your thoughts, you will realize how important it is to think about what you are thinking about. While you cannot control your circumstances, you are 100% responsible for your thought life. You are responsible for what you think about and choose to believe. Choose wisely, choose to think the truth and shut out the lies that you are not good enough, pretty enough or smart enough.

Your mind is extremely powerful, you need to make that power work for you and not against you. The battle for your dreams and purpose is fought in your mind first. If you can't win in your mind, you can't win in life.

If you want to be able to succeed in your Five Non-Negotiables, you first have to believe that you can and tear down any negative thoughts that are holding you back. Your thoughts control your behavior, so it is crucial that you have control over your thoughts.

> **Your Turn**
>
> I know that there has been a lot of science in this chapter, but are you starting to realize just how powerful your thoughts are? Write down a couple things that have stood out to you in this chapter so far regarding the power of your mind.

How To Set Your Mind Free

You have the ability to unlock that prison door and get out. You have to make a choice to do it though and stick with it until you are completely free. You set your mind free by:

1. First learning the truth, it is the truth that sets you free. You must wake up and realize that your mind is a prison because of the lies you've been believing. You need to recognize those lies.

   If you believed that you, "can't change your bad habit" and you now recognize that this is a lie, then you would replace your negative thought with a new one. Your new thought might be, "I can change my habit because I can do anything that I set my mind to. I am powerful and I will do it."

2. You need to renew your mind everyday with the truth. That means replacing the negative lies with positive truths. Just knowing the truth is not enough, you need to act on it by consistently applying the truth to your mind by meditating on it and correcting your negative thoughts and replacing them with positive thoughts.

   So whenever those negative, "I can't do it" thoughts creep in, you would replace them with the positive thoughts. Also, you should set aside time each day to think about the positive thoughts. Don't just wait for the negative thoughts to happen so you can knock them down, also proactively set aside time to think about the positive thoughts as well.

Each day when you are doing Non-Negotiable #1: Reviewing Your Goals Daily, you are literally renewing your mind and reshaping the physical structure of your brain. You are waking up your DNA and unlocking the power of your brain to help you accomplish your goal.

The more emotion that is tied to your why, the greater priority that your brain will assign to helping you accomplish your goals.

3. You need to keep doing this over and over until you have destroyed the lie and you confidently walk in the truth.

   Changing your mindset can be easy at the beginning, but then we tend to forget about it and get lazy with our minds again and the next thing you know we are back in prison again. Setting aside specific time to practice thinking your new thoughts needs to become non-negotiable.

4. You need to take action on the truth by starting to do the things that align with the truth. Now that you realize that the thought, "you can't change your bad habit" is a lie, it is time to start physically changing the habit. Setting a goal and sticking with it.

Your mind was created to dream big, love big and forgive big. Your mind was created so that you could think amazing thoughts and then use the power of your mind to turn those thoughts into a reality. Your mind is a powerful tool and what you think you will become and do.

Your Turn

What is a lie that you are struggling with right now in your mind?

How is believing this lie affecting your life?

Why have you believed this lie?

What is the truth about that lie?

How are you going to stop believing this lie and replace it with the truth?

Do something physically to help you remember to continue combatting this lie. Maybe ask a friend to hold you accountable so that anytime you talk about it they remind you to stop. You could put a sticky note on your mirror to remind you to change your thoughts or set a little reminder on your phone. Just do something to help remind you to start combatting this lie. Once you have physically done something write "My mind is powerful and I am going to use that power for good" in the space below.

The Five Non-Negotiables

Controlling your mind and using it to build your life, faith, family and others is what it is meant for. Your mind was never created for negativity or self-hate.

Using your mind correctly is the key to unlocking so many wonderful things in your life. Your mind is a powerful tool that God gave you to create the life you were born to live. Stop using your mind for other purposes that are not serving you.

When you turn that powerful gift against yourself that same amazing power begins to tear you down. Your thoughts are powerful no matter what you think so just as they are equally powerful in building you up, they are equally powerful in tearing you down.

It's time to take that power back and start using it for good.

Non-Negotiable #3

Personal Growth

13

Non-Negotiable #3:
Personal Growth

"The only person you are destined to become, is the person you decide to be."

-Ralph Waldo Emerson

What Is Personal Growth

Personal growth is taking time to improve who you are on the inside whether that be your habits, mindset or beliefs. It is continuing to work on yourself to develop your full potential so that you can fulfill your life's purpose.

There are so many voices in the world trying to tell us who we are supposed to be, what we are supposed to look like, what success is. We cannot rely on culture or others opinions to lead us to our purpose and identity.

Your personal growth time allows you to shut the world out and recenter your life on the things that truly matter most. It is a time to evaluate your mindset and habits and focus on improving who you are on the inside.

When we set aside time for personal growth we are really setting aside the time we need to:

- Get our thoughts under control.
- Learn new things and expand our minds.
- Pray and meditate.
- Calm down and recenter ourselves.
- Be grateful and take a minute to appreciate what we have.
- Set goals and evaluate our progress.
- Shift our energy and flow of our entire day to a more positive one.
- Be still and connect with God.

This is only a short list of the things our personal growth time is meant for, but as you can see these are not small things. Pretty much everything we do in life flows out from who we are on the inside, so it is extremely important to take time to nourish, grow and develop our inside.

I didn't want to call this non-negotiable "Spiritual Growth" because it is more than just that, but a huge part of my personal growth is actually focusing on my spiritual growth. It is my time to read my Bible, pray and connect with God. Spiritual growth is by far the most important piece to my personal growth, but it is not the only piece.

I remember one time I was having a bad day and I wasn't in the best mood and Reese said to me, "Mom, maybe you need to go have some quiet time with Jesus." At five years old she recognized how important personal growth time was for me and it's affect on my entire attitude throughout the day.

Personal growth can look different depending on what season of life you are in. Some seasons might require you to work on patience, while others might require you to learn to control your emotions or grow in forgiveness.

Whatever the season of life you are in, there is always a need for personal growth.

Some personal growth happens through life experiences that force us to mature, but there is a lot of personal growth that can only come from our own purposeful efforts to proactively grow. When it comes to personal growth, the possibilities are endless. You can grow and learn as much as you want throughout your lifetime.

What you can't do is stay the same and expect to start living out your goals and dreams. You must grow on the inside long before you see the changes on the outside.

Why We Don't Take Time For Personal Growth

Personal growth tends to get the backseat in our lives because it can feel selfish to take time for ourselves. It also doesn't produce immediate tangible results and in our generation of quick fixes and microwaved meals we don't think we have the time to wait.

In many seasons of my life I struggled with making time for personal growth because everything else felt so much more important. I didn't make time to consistently pursue personal growth so I didn't realize the value that it would bring to my life.

You just finished reading a whole chapter on mindset which showed you just how powerful your mind is. It literally controls your entire life: what you think, say and do.

Well, it is during your personal growth time that you start to reshape your thoughts. It is during that time that you start harnessing the power of your mind. This is important stuff and you need to be making time for it.

Let's take a minute to talk about some of the personal growth areas that we should work on.

Your Turn

Do you currently set aside regular time for personal growth?

If you do then what do you normally do during that time? If you don't, what would you like to do during your personal growth time?

Areas Of Personal Growth To Work On
Self-Image

Your self-image is called, "image" because it literally represents the image or picture that you have of yourself on the inside. Everything we say, think and do is a reflection of this picture.

Unfortunately, throughout life we have had many negative words spoken to us that have shaped parts of our self-image in a negative way. If we never make time for personal growth, then we will be stuck thinking and believing whatever our life experiences have told us and the words others have spoken to us.

Most often people feel that they are a victim of their self image, as if it is a picture someone else (such as their parents) drew for them and they have no control over it. Other people feel stuck in a poor self image because of something from their past. It is as if a snapshot from a past moment in time has become the only image they now see of themselves on a daily basis.

The truth is that those things in your past do not define you or determine your value. You are the artist in the picture of your life and you get to determine what the final product is. You have control over your own self-image, therefore, you also have the ability to change it if you don't like it.

That is what personal growth is all about. It is about updating the portrait you have stuck in your mind about yourself to the correct image.

What you believe about yourself will become your reality. That is why it is extremely important to spend time evaluating and adjusting our beliefs about ourselves. When it comes to our self-image, we need to only believe the truth and all lies must go.

Lies

Lies spoken to you by others and lies you have spoken to yourself, they all need to go. You need to be a careful gatekeeper of your mind and only allow the truth in. Block out the lies because once you let them in, they begin to shape your life.

The list of lies we believe about ourselves seems endless, but I have taken the liberty to write out a few below.

- I can't ever change. I just don't have the ability to stay consistent and stick to my goals. I will always be this way.
- One day my life will be happy, but I can't be happy now because I don't have _____ yet.
- I can never be who I really want to be because I have a horrible past or have made major mistakes.
- I can't succeed because I don't have the right connections, family or finances.
- I have a big mouth and I just can't help it, it is just who I am.
- I don't have self-control.
- Habits and mindsets might work for others, but it won't work for me.
- I have tried and failed so many times, there is no point in trying again. I already know I will fail again.
- This is so much easier for everyone else than it is for me.
- I was born this way, there is nothing I can do about it.

The Five Non-Negotiables

I want you to be real vulnerable and open with yourself in this chapter so that we can do some deep work on the inside. I am not going to ask you to do something that I would not do myself, so let me share some of the lies that I struggle with.

I struggle with believing that I need to stress out about something or it won't get done. I know this sounds strange, but I am addicted to stress. If I am not stressed out about something then I just don't feel normal.

Rather than getting to work on a project or task, I have to stress out about it first in my mind. I am so used to living with this underlying stress that I don't even hardly recognize it anymore.

I believe that if I am not stressed out about something then I won't have the motivation to get it done. This belief robs me of a lot of joy. Things that I am meant to enjoy and appreciate can easily become burdens and overwhelming to me because I choose to stress about them.

I also struggle with feeling like I'm not good enough. I know to you this might sound silly, but to me, unfortunately it has been my truth for almost my entire life. Remember that hamster wheel that we talked about a few chapters back? Well I am a pro at waking up each day and immediately jumping on that wheel and running as hard as I can so that I can prove to myself and to everyone else that I am good enough.

It took me a long time to recognize that I was living my whole life and daily schedule based on one big fat lie, that I wasn't good enough. Once I realized I had been lying to myself for all of these years I got mad. My time is valuable and it is one of the few things that I can never get back and I was wasting it on a lie. Ugh.

I want to live a life where my schedule and goals are based on my purpose which is loving God, loving and serving my family, writing this book and whatever else God wants to do with the gifts and dreams He has put on my heart.

I don't want to wake up and spend all I have trying to impress others and prove my worth to them. I discovered this lie during my personal growth time. God spoke it to my heart and opened my eyes to see that I don't have anything to prove.

I wish I could tell you that in that moment everything changed for me, but it didn't. It was in that moment that I finally saw the truth of my motives and actions, I finally recognized the lie, but knowing the truth wasn't enough.

It was only by showing up the next day for my personal growth time and studying the truth about my worth that I started to break down the lie.

Then I showed up again the next day for my personal growth time and started changing my heart and mindset just a tiny bit more. Then I showed up the next day and the next until my personal growth time became a non-negotiable in my life.

I started making personal growth time a priority and set aside time several days a week to focus on it. I declared war on the lies in my mind by physically showing up to fight them with the truth.

I have kept at defeating this lie for a few years now and while I still struggle with people's opinions at times, they truly matter so much less now.

I am experiencing more and more freedom in this area and I never want to go back to that version of myself that was a slave to the opinions of others. The only way I am getting free is by showing up consistently for my personal growth time and seeking after the truth and the freedom that comes from the truth.

If I had not consistently set aside time to work on who I am on the inside, I would still be running on that same hamster wheel. I would be wearing myself out in hopes that someone would look my way and make me feel worthy. No more, I am done with that wheel.

Your Turn

I have given you a list of lies above to get you started thinking, but now it is time to get real and be vulnerable. What lies have you believed about yourself that are you struggling with right now? Can you relate to any of these lies above or are there other lies that you have been believing? Write these lies out in detail.

How do these lies speak to you? Through your mind, media, friends, yourself or co-workers? Where is the majority of the lies coming from?

What does their voice sound like?

How do they make you feel?

Is there a specific moment that you can look back on that you realize you started believing these lies? Or have you been believing these for so long you can't remember when they started?

Self-Talk

You are the most influential person in your life. It is not the external circumstances around you that have the greatest impact on who you are, it is your own self-talk.

While the external circumstances around you affect you, it is your own SELF that determines the degree of impact that those circumstances will have on you.

You probably don't even realize it, but you talk to yourself all day long. In the words of the best-selling mindset author Joyce Meyer, "It is time to start thinking about what we are thinking about!" How are you talking to yourself each day?

My self-talk was a big hindrance for me when I was getting started with my non-negotiables. I kept saying to myself that there was no way that I was actually going to be able to stick with my non-negotiables.

I had set goals and failed so many times. During my depression I had proved to myself over and over again that I didn't have self-control and discipline. These past failures translated into hopelessness for my future in my mind.

This negative self-talk made it so hard to stick with my goals because although I wanted to keep them and I set all the plans in place to accomplish them, there was a constant voice in the back of my head telling me, "This is a total waste of time, you will never stick with it. You can't do this Chelsea, you just aren't consistent enough, I mean look at your last goal, you didn't even make it a month at that goal. You can't even get yourself to consistently floss your teeth, how do you think you will ever get your eating under control or actually go to the gym consistently?"

Every single time I would try to show up for a goal, that negative voice would be screaming in my head trying to get me to give up and quit because deep on the inside I believed I couldn't do it. I have these same voices screaming at me just like you, we all do.

The Five Non-Negotiables

We all have to overcome many things to fulfill our purpose and setting aside time consistently to tackle ourselves head on and grow on the inside is the only way we are going to get there. Personal growth is a non-negotiable if you want to live your life with purpose and fulfill your potential.

Your self-talk should actually be a chance to encourage, motivate and stir up hope inside yourself. Your self-talk should not have room for negativity, criticism, comparison, guilt and fear. What you speak into yourself everyday will determine your future.

We want to blame what others have said to us in the past and the labels they have put on us for the reasons we are struggling in life, but we never want to blame our own self-talk. It is so much easier to point the finger at others. The truth is, that if you speak positively to yourself, then it won't even matter what others say about you, you will know who you truly are and that will be enough.

I am not saying that other people's words don't hurt and that they have not contributed in big ways to our own hurt and struggles. What I am saying is that when we believe the negative things others have spoken over us and start to repeat them to ourselves daily we make the damage so much worse.

Do you realize that just because someone says something bad about you, you don't have to believe it? Why can it be so much easier to believe negative lies that people say to us over compliments people give us?

When we forget that we have the power to control what we will and will not receive in our minds, we end up letting the negative words in and sometimes we even begin repeating them to ourselves.

You need to be your number one cheerleader, not your number one critic. If there are things that you don't like about yourself, stop beating yourself up over them everyday through your self-talk and actually DO something to change those things about yourself. Continuing to speak negatively about it to yourself day in and day out is not going to do anything good for you, instead choose to make a change in that area.

I remember one time when I was in college and I got stuck with an early morning class. I hated waking up so early and quietly walking down the dormroom halls while all my other friends were fast asleep. So I started to complain about it everyday. I would complain to anyone in my dorm that would listen to me.

After a couple weeks one of the girls said, "If you aren't happy about your early morning class then just change your schedule." Another girl standing next to her looked me straight in the eye and said, "Yes if you don't like it then just do something about it, but if you aren't going to do anything about it then please shut up about it already."

At first I was a little offended, but then I realized they were right. I was complaining about something that I had total control over. I ended up going straight to the counselors office and changed my class to the afternoon time and I was one happy camper.

As a loving friend I am looking you in the eye and saying, "If you don't like something about your life, then change it." Stop berating yourself about it, stop complaining to others about it and just do something about it.

That is what your personal growth time is for, to do something about who you are on the inside.

Your Turn

What is some of the negative self-talk that you have with yourself? Write out a typical conversation in your mind.

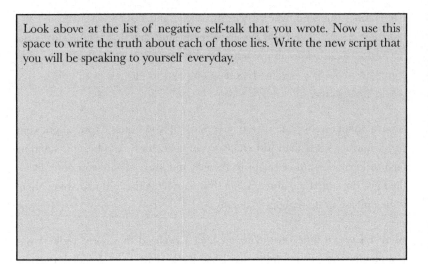

Look above at the list of negative self-talk that you wrote. Now use this space to write the truth about each of those lies. Write the new script that you will be speaking to yourself everyday.

Perspective

When you are first beginning to make changes you have to start with the same set of circumstances you have been caught in for a while.

For example, if you want to lose 100 lbs you don't automatically get a 50 lb loss head start because you finally decided to start losing the weight. No, you have to start with all 100 lbs to lose.

The difference between the last twenty times you tried and failed and this time is going to be your perspective. This time you are going to start with a positive attitude and belief that you really can lose those 100 lbs.

If you keep looking at your circumstances through the same negative and self-defeating lens and if you keep up with all the negative self-talk then you will make it twice as hard to reach your goals.

Stand back from the situation and think about how you have been thinking about it. Are you negative? Are you already convinced it won't work this time because it hasn't worked in the past? Do you see the same limitations clouding your motivation as you have every other time you have tried to lose the weight?

You need to stop and rethink your circumstances from a new lens, gain a new perspective. Maybe some of the things you saw as a negative can actually be a positive if you look at it from a new angle.

Don't set the same goals with the same old perspective. Set the same goal you have set many times before, but this time look at it in a new way. You cannot move forward into your future trying to accomplish new things with old mindsets.

Your Turn

Write out one of your goals you have already set during the course of this book.

What are some of the negative perspectives that you have been taking along with you while trying to reach this goal?

What is a new perspective that you can now have about reaching this goal?

Tools To Help You With Personal Growth

This non-negotiable is all about setting time aside to consistently work on personal growth. This can mean taking time to focus on growing in your self-talk, overcoming particular insecurities or changing your perspective on your circumstances. Whatever area you know needs some personal time and attention.

Personal growth is a very personal journey, but I want to give you a few ideas of things you can do to work on your personal growth during the time you have set aside. Below are a few ideas to get you started on your personal growth journey.

- **Read** - If you struggle to find time to read, consider an audiobook. Listen while you drive to help reset your mind and attitude for that day.

- **Meditate or Pray** - Quiet your heart and mind. Bring all your cares to God.

- **Podcasts** - Similar to books, these are helpful when it comes to adjusting your attitude and perspective on life. The nice thing about podcasts is that if you are short on time, you can listen to ten minute episodes.

  Listen to them while you are getting ready in the morning, driving your car or folding the laundry.

- **Journal** - Write out how you are feeling, your prayers, your goals or whatever topic is on your mind.

- **Read the Bible** - I know that not everyone who reads this book is a Christian, but I would be remiss if I did not mention this idea of reading the Bible for personal growth. In fact, a lot of the Bible is simply God reminding us about our worth, value and identity.

  There are so many amazing truths and insights in the Bible and I feel so strongly about the huge impact that knowing God has had on my life that I felt like it would not be fair for me to give you all this other advice and completely leave out the part that has had the biggest impact on my life. I feel like if we have made it this far together on this journey then we have reached the friend status and as your friend I can't leave out the best part!

What I am encouraging you to do in this non-negotiable is to set time aside consistently whether that be once a week, once a day, whatever you decide, but set a specific amount of time on a regular basis to focus on your personal growth.

You need to make spending time working on your personal growth a consistent, non-negotiable, habit.

Your Turn

It is time to set a new habit in your life. Make a commitment today that you are going to set aside time regularly for personal growth. Use the space below to write out your goal for personal growth. Include how often you plan on setting aside time for personal growth and how long each personal growth time will be. For example: I am going to spend twenty minutes working on personal growth three days per week.

You know what I am going to ask you to do now... your why. Why are you going to make personal growth non-negotiable in your life? Take your time to dig deep and answer this question. You need to know exactly why it is worth taking time you would be spending on something else to slow down and work on who you are on the inside.

Put your new non-negotiable goal for personal growth in your phone or wherever you have your goals so that you can easily review them each day when the alarm goes off. Be sure to include your why as well, this new goal will need to be reviewed daily just like the other non-negotiables. Once you have added your personal growth goal, write, "I am going to prioritize my personal growth because my life's purpose depends on it" below.

List below what you will do during your personal growth time (hint, you can use some of the ideas above).

Get out your calendar and schedule the exact days and times that you will be working on your personal growth. Make sure you have it set up so that you can do this regularly. Whether it is everyday, once a week, whatever the amount of time, get it scheduled right now. Write, "I am excited to grow on the inside" below once it is scheduled.

Your last step is to get prepared. If there is a book you want to read and you don't own it then order it right now. If there is a podcast you want to listen to then set it up in your phone and download it now. If there is a group you want to join, do the research right now and reach out to them and figure out how you can get plugged in right away. If you are going to start journaling then make sure you have a journal.

Do not delay, even though your personal growth time might not be scheduled until next week, do everything you can to be fully prepared so that when the day comes for you to start working on your personal growth you can start immediately. Once you have done everything you can to be fully prepared for your personal growth time write, "I am fully prepared to change my life" below.

14

Embrace The Suck

"The one who does most to avoid suffering is, in the end, the one who suffers the most."

-Thomas Merton

The military has a great quote and at my CrossFit gym we often steal it to help get us through our workouts. It simply says, "Embrace the suck."

The urban dictionary defines this phrase as:

> *To consciously accept or appreciate something that is extremely unpleasant, but unavoidable for forward progress.*

This basically means that if you want to move forward you must go through or overcome things that are going to suck. Therefore, you might as well embrace it rather than fight it.

Stop Hating It And Start Embracing It

Your purpose is on the other side of a whole lot of steps that suck. To become the person who has their priorities straight and who lives without negotiating, you must go through a ton of things that suck. The problem is that in this day and age we have been taught to hate the suck. We run as fast and far from the pain and struggle as we possibly can.

We view the suck in a negative way. Struggle is something to avoid. Commitment and dedication is too hard. This mentality of viewing the suck as a negative has made us weak and unable to do hard things. The truth is that life is made of lots of hard things. We need to stop spending our lives running from hard things and look them square in the eye and take them on. Every single life of greatness was built on struggle, sacrifice and commitment.

It is in the constant daily grind of choosing the hard thing over and over that we build great lives of purpose. So if you want to live out your purpose, you must endure the suck so you might as well start embracing it. Stop seeing it as a negative thing and start seeing it as a positive thing.

Your Turn

Are you somebody who embraces the suck or someone who runs from it?

What areas do you tend to run from the suck and what areas do you tend to embrace the suck?

Motivation And Opportunities

The more suck in your life, the more opportunities you have to grow. Stop spending your life looking for loopholes and shortcuts and quick fixes. Look at what you need to get done and just go do it.

Learn to let the pain of the struggle become a motivator, not a hindrance. Stop being motivated only by the things that are easy, comfortable and quick. Save those things for the mediocre, but that is not you. You are not mediocre so stop living that way.

If you want to get stronger, be healthier, have control over your finances and put your family and faith first then you will have to fight for that life every single day. That life will not be handed to you.

No one can make that life happen for you, except you. So it is time to start seeing the struggle for what it really is, an opportunity to grow. A stepping stone that gets you closer to your goal. A life lesson to be learned and wisdom to be gained.

Part of what you gain from doing hard things is discovering that you really can do them. This gives you the confidence to continue to push yourself to grow. When I went on that sugar fast for ninety days I didn't think I had the willpower to do it. Once I accomplished it I gained confidence in myself and it gave me the courage to take on other challenges that I had been avoiding.

Having confidence in yourself and knowing that you have the discipline to accomplish hard things is important. That confidence can only come from going through hard things though. When you refuse to take on a challenge because you accept it as too hard, you are selling yourself short. Stop doing this.

If you want to run from something, run from mediocrity. If you want to hate something, hate mediocrity. Don't hate the struggle, don't run from the hard stuff. Those are the things that make you great.

The Five Non-Negotiables

Greatness is not some destination that you finally reach at the end of your life. Greatness is an accumulation of a life lived great. That means waking up each and every day prepared to embrace the struggle and fight for who you are and your purpose on this earth.

So don't you dare hit that snooze button, get your butt out of bed and go do your workout. Stop waiting for all the stars to align to work on your goals or reprioritize your life.

Whatever you do, do not make the mistake of thinking that these Five Non-Negotiables are going to be easy. Take on only one non-negotiable at a time if you have to, but don't you dare quit because it gets hard. If it is getting hard then that is probably a sign that you are doing the right things.

If you are reading this book then the chances are that you need this in your life right now. So when it gets tough, overwhelming and hard, don't you dare quit. You need this, you can do this. Let the struggle become part of your motivation. It's time to change your mindset, the struggle is good, the easy way out is bad.

You can do this. You have made it this far in the book, you are making forward progress in becoming who you are born to be. Keep embracing the suck, the life you were made for is on the other side of it so keep going. You got this!

Your Turn

Are you committed to start embracing the suck?

What is one thing that you know you should be doing but you have been avoiding because it will suck to do? It can be anything from cleaning out your garage, to setting up a meeting with someone you need to talk with, to forgiving someone or writing a nice card to someone. Pick something you know you should do but you have been procrastinating at.

You don't think that I am going to let you off the hook in a chapter about embracing the suck without actually making you embrace it. Pull out your calendar and schedule in a time that you are going to work on the thing you listed above within the next 72 hours.

You don't have to complete it within the next 72 hours, but you need to get started on it by then. Schedule it now and don't skip it because it sucks to do. Instead see this as a chance to embrace the suck because not only are you going to get the sucky task over with, but you will be even stronger because you embraced a struggle instead of running from it. That is the type of person you want to be, so set a date in your calendar to do it and then go do it. Once you have it scheduled write, "I love embracing the suck because it makes me stronger" below.

You Are Doing It!

I know that at this point in the book I have asked you to do a lot of things. I hope that you are not feeling overwhelmed. My intent is not to stress you out with too many things to do. What I want to do is to help you reorder your life according to the things that matter most.

Reorganizing your life around a new set of priorities takes time and a lot of work, but I promise you that it will all be worth it. It's okay if you only want to tackle one non-negotiable at a time. All that matters is that you're taking steps forward in your life. Go at the pace that's best for you.

The Five Non-Negotiables

Look at how far you have come already. You have set new goals, learned how to review them daily, attached a why to your goals for motivation. You have made progress in your health and tackled some wrong mindsets. You have set alarms and reminders to keep you going and have finally started making personal growth time a priority in your life.

You have already accomplished so much. I just want you to take a minute to recognize all the amazing work you are doing in your life. Look at how much action you have taken towards becoming the person you want to be.

These are all really important changes that you are making and I am so happy for you. Especially if you are actually doing all the "Your Turns" in the book. The whole point of this book is to get you to take action and if you are doing that then you should stop right now and congratulate yourself. You are doing the hard work to better your life. I am so proud of you.

You are embracing the suck!

15

Excuses

"Excuses will always be there for you, opportunity won't."

-Unknown

Oh boy do we have excuses: the list of reasons why we can't do something. In fact you may have already had many running through your head while reading this book. Your mind is panicking as you hear the words "no" and "neglect." It tells you things like:

- I am too busy, there is no way I can squeeze more into my schedule.
- This crazy lady just doesn't understand because her life isn't as hard as mine.
- Maybe I could actually change my life if I had more money or a better job.
- This is so much harder for me than it is for everyone else.

When we are having a moment full of motivation we think, "I am never going to let anyone stand between me and my goals", but when push comes to shove we let excuses stand in the way. We won't let someone else get in our way, we are far too stubborn for that, but we will let ourselves get in our own way.

The bottom line is, you can have a life of excuses or a life of purpose, but you can't have both. So it is up to you to decide. Stop fooling yourself into believing you can have both, that is a lie.

Excuses are some of the biggest growth stunters in the world. They hold you back from your potential. They weaken you in every way: mentally, emotionally, spiritually and physically. Excuses basically allow us to excuse away our potential. It's time we start seeing excuses for what they really are: lies.

You would never want to keep a friend around who lied to you all the time, yet we have become best friends with excuses and accepted the lie that these excuses justify our lack of growth and personal responsibility.

I am begging you to break off your endearing friendship with excuses. Growing is painful, taking personal responsibility and walking through hard things is tough, but I promise you it is worth it.

With growth and maturity comes freedom and wisdom. Don't make a deal with yourself that forfeits maturity for comfort. That is a bad deal.

The list of excuses is endless. While I definitely don't have enough paper to address them all, let's talk about a few excuses that are holding us back.

Common Excuses

I Don't Have Time

Time is the great equalizer. We each have different talents, incomes, families, abilities, upbringings and so on, but every single one of us has the exact same 24 hours each day. The difference between those who accomplish their dreams and those who do not is how they spend their 24 hours.

The Law of Forced Efficiency states, "There is never enough time to do everything, but there is always enough time to do the most important thing." Your list of things to do will always be there, the key is to sift through the unimportant and be sure to tackle the most important tasks first.

The problem is we are experts at living busy, jam-packed, over scheduled lives, yet at the end of the day when we put our head on the pillow can we really say that we did a great deal towards achieving our goals and purpose?

You have the gift of 24 hours in every day of your life; never more, never less. These 24 hours are extremely precious, yet we treat them so cavalier. We have huge dreams and goals, yet we forget to use the gift of time to accomplish them.

Time is not some obscure, untouchable and uncontrollable force out there that evades us each day as we try to accomplish our long "to do" list. No, time is a real thing, it is the same every day, we can count on it, we can manage it, we can own it, we can make it work for us and not against us. You can gain control over your time! Time does not control you.

Dave Ramsey has a lesson he teaches in regards to budgeting money that I have applied to managing my time. Dave teaches that you need to spend all of your money on paper before you ever spend it in person. Meaning if I am going to make $2,000 next week, then I need to plan out where every single dollar will go before it hits my bank account.

I might assign $200 for my savings, $500 for my rent, $50 for groceries and so on until I have allocated every dollar. The point is that before I ever spend a dime in person, I have already planned where my money will go. Then once I receive my paycheck I just follow the plan and if I stick to it I will reach my financial goals.

This is how I spend my time, I budget it. Each minute of my 24 hours is assigned a specific purpose. I start with the most important items on my list and schedule those first. Next, I schedule in all the rest.

The Five Non-Negotiables

I know what you are thinking. Life isn't perfect and you can't follow an exact script when it comes to your daily schedule. I hear you, life does tend to send us a lot of curveballs. There are probably more days where my schedule doesn't go 100% as I planned than actually does.

The perfect schedule is not the goal, making sure the most important things get done each day is. But when you have a plan, even when things don't go 100% according to your plan you will probably still end up much closer to reaching your goals than if you just meander through the day from thing to thing without planning time for your goals.

Even if I only got twenty minutes of my workout in instead of a whole hour, I still did a lot better than if I hadn't even scheduled in my workout at all.

I understand that just because you plan out your day, it doesn't mean that everything will go according to your wonderful plan. The point is not making your life perfect, it is making it purposeful. Planning ahead will bring a lot more purpose into how you use your time and on the days that life is just too crazy to stick to the schedule that's ok. At least you have many other days where you are able to work on your goals. You will be making progress.

Have you ever looked back at the end of the month and wondered where all your money went? The same thing will keep happening with your time unless you start budgeting it. Time will keep slipping through your fingers. On the other hand, just as investing your money wisely can give you great gains, investing your time wisely will yield great gains and rewards for your future.

Your Turn

Make a list of the most important things that you need to accomplish tomorrow. Do you have appointments, a workout or meetings that you can't miss? Don't forget about your goals, too. Write them all below.

Now use the calendar provided below to fill in all of your most important tasks that you listed above in the corresponding time period. I have given you half hour increments.

5:00 AM

5:30 AM

6:00 AM

6:30 AM

7:00 AM

7:30 AM

8:00 AM

8:30 AM

9:00 AM

9:30 AM

10:00 AM

10:30 AM

11:00 AM

11:30 AM

12:00 PM

The Five Non-Negotiables

| 12:30 PM |
| 1:00 PM |
| 1:30 PM |
| 2:00 PM |
| 2:30 PM |
| 3:00 PM |
| 3:30 PM |
| 4:00 PM |
| 4:30 PM |
| 5:00 PM |
| 5:30 PM |
| 6:00 PM |
| 6:30 PM |
| 7:00 PM |
| 7:30 PM |
| 8:00 PM |
| 8:30 PM |
| 9:00 PM |
| 9:30 PM |
| 10:00 PM |

Now go through the rest of your day and budget every minute of it. Time to make dinner, special time with your kids, time for laundry and dishes and running errands. Fill every minute of your day up strategically with the things that need to get done and that matter most to you.

Budgeting your time is not meant to become an insane taskmaster that you have to stick to every second, it is supposed to be a tool to help direct your day and bring your purpose into it. Schedule rest time, fun time and friend time. Filling up every minute of your schedule does not necessarily mean filling up every minute with work. It just means making sure each minute has a purpose.

If you need rest, schedule it in, if you want some creative time to paint or decorate, schedule it in. By scheduling your time you are making your time work for you and you are choosing to fill your life with your priorities instead of wandering from thing to thing everyday.

Again, this is not meant to become your taskmaster that you stress over every minute of your day and feel pressure to stay perfectly on schedule. It is meant to help you regain control of how you are spending your time and find ways to fit the things that matter to you most into your daily life.

Once your calendar is completely full write, "I make my time work for me because I budget it" below.

I usually budget my whole week at once, I just wanted you to start with one day so that it isn't too overwhelming. Continue to do this each night before bed so your next day is already planned out for you and once you get the hang of it you can start planning out each week ahead of time.

Be sure to include time in your schedule for tomorrow to plan for the next day. It will only take a few minutes, but schedule it in so you have a set time to plan for the next day.

I know I have already said this, but one last time: do not let this schedule make you feel restricted and stressed out. Budgeting your time is about regaining control over your time and assigning purpose to it so that at the end of the day you make time for the most important things.

If scheduling every minute stresses you out then just make sure you schedule in the most important things and leave the rest blank. Remember to schedule in rest time and downtime. Basically use your time to create the life you want instead of letting time slip away.

Life is not perfect and many days won't go exactly as you budgeted for them to go. That is OK. But you have a much better chance of accomplishing your goals and living out your priorities if you schedule specific time to accomplish them.

Use your time budget as a guide, not as a task master.

I Never Finish What I Start

"I always start things, but I never finish them. This is just going to be a waste of my time because I will never follow through and complete this."

This excuse has held me back many times because as soon as I believe that there is no point in trying to make a change I am defeated before I even get started. Even if I do have the drive to actually get started, this excuse is a negative voice in my head that keeps sucking the hope that I will ever really change out of me.

This is an excuse that you need to tackle by being honest. The truth that I speak to myself is, "Maybe I haven't been able to make this change before, maybe I have tried twenty times and failed every time, but the odds for success are in my favor now. I can change and I will change and I will not let my past failures hold me back from my future success."

Your truth might be worded differently than mine, but you get the point. So what? You failed multiple times, most people don't get it right the first time anyways. Let the past go and move forward. If our past mistakes determined our future then we would never have a good future. Your future is not based on the decisions you made in the past, they are based on the decisions you make right now.

Believing that you are wasting your time by trying to make a positive change in your life is a complete lie. Every minute you spend working towards changing your life is a victory. If you exchange your excuses for effort you will change your life.

Getting started is hard, because in the beginning we are building a foundation. Foundations are not exciting. They are essential, but they are also boring. We want to do the great things, the fun shiny things immediately, but unfortunately we need to get the basics down first.

Having a season in life of focusing on the basics is like building a tall tower. When you build a tower you have seasons of:

- Drafting the plans (planning out how you want your house to be built in detail.)
- Breaking ground (taking the first step of change.)
- Digging out for the foundation (digging out the junk and paving the way for the new.)
- Carefully laying the foundation (get started building.)

Finally, after months and months of planning, digging and cement laying that you finally begin to see the signs of a real building being erected. Even then, it is just a shell of what it is dreamed to be. Only boards and beams.

Then carefully piece by piece it is erected. It is not until all the essentials get done and the foundation is properly laid that you get to start painting and decorating and making it look pretty. We want to look like a beautifully decorated house without having to do the work of building a foundation. We want to skip to the part where we look pretty and organized.

I am going to be completely honest with you right now. I am sitting in my bed typing this book thinking about how much I don't like parts of this process. It's my own dang book and there are still parts of the Five Non-Negotiables that I just want to erase and pretend like I don't need to apply it to my life. This process is hard, I am going through this with you.

When I write this stuff I get convicted of my own lack of consistency and my own excuses. I don't like facing the truths about my mis-prioritized daily life, my comfort zone, the bad habits that are easy and I am accustomed too. This dang book, this dang process is literally asking me to make changes that affect my everyday life... I don't want to change my everyday life. I want to stay where I am.

Yet at the same time there is a voice from deep within me screaming for change at the top of its lungs. Through the excuses and self doubt and failures of my past I have learned to turn a deaf ear to it. Yet somehow this voice has refused to relent and in the moments that I am still I can faintly hear it. It is screaming at me to go for it, to be all that I can be. To dare to jump off the cliff and change my habits. To see what life is really like on the other side. To be brave and do hard things.

You see I can't write this book and talk about it, I can't lead anyone if I am not living this myself. Ugh... this means that if you are reading this then you are not in this alone. I am right here with you. If I can do it, trust me you can do it too.

Your Turn

Write your own truth that you will speak to yourself whenever you struggle with the thoughts that you are a quitter and you will never succeed at making these changes in your life. What is the truth that you are going to speak to those lies? Write it out below in detail and mark this page so you can come back to it on days you are struggling with doubting yourself.

Life Changes Only Happen To Others, Not Me

You are where you are right now as a result of the choices you have made. In other words, you are not where you are because that's just how life is, or because you didn't win the lottery or because of some supernatural force that is out of your control. You are where you are because of the choices you made.

The good news is that if you don't like where you are, then you can make new choices and change your life. You determine your future, you determine your destiny. While there are many things that life throws at us that are out of our control, we still have the choice of how we are going to respond to them.

You have to dig deep and find the courage to overcome obstacles in life. You need to recognize your power. You are truly powerful and your life has the ability to make an incredible impact on this world for the good. That is not only true for those born rich, extra smart, gifted, popular or come from the "right" family. That is true for everyone.

You are powerful, stop giving your power away to excuses and wrong thinking. Your life will be changed if you choose to stop making excuses and start exercising your power of choice in a positive and productive way.

I have had seasons where my choices were not good, I mean really not good. I look back now and I can hardly believe how low I got at times. I went through six years of depression that put me in a hole that was deep and dark. I was drowning in misery, depression and loneliness. I would look at others who had their lives together and I would feel like I could never be like them. The more I looked at others around me who seemed so happy the worse I felt about myself.

Then one day I stopped looking at other people and their perfect little lives and I started looking at myself. The truth is I hit rock bottom and I knew I was at a point in my life where I either found the strength to make the necessary changes in my life, or I would lose myself completely.

I knew I was capable of more, but I had sat in depression for so many years that I had forgotten who I really was. I was a mere shadow of who I was created to be, miserable and hating myself.

I wish I could tell you some miraculous story about how my life instantly turned around, but the truth is I made a choice that I was going to change and for once in my life I stuck with it.

Each day I focused on the choices I could make and not the unattainable perfect life of others around me. What choice can I make today to get me one step closer to getting out of this hole was the question I tried to answer everyday? Each day I climbed out just a little bit more.

To be honest, there were many times that I would take one step forward and two steps backward, but I just kept at it. Doing everything right was not the key to making it out of the hole, but rather it was the choice to NOT GIVE UP! Once you find the courage to not give up and dig yourself out of a hole like that, you know that you can do anything.

I know how hard this is, I know the struggle with self-doubt, fear, depression and lethargy. I know how it feels to be lonely and anxious and completely lost.

I want you to know that I am here with you on this journey. I don't want to just give you a bunch of advice, I want this book to spur you to believe in yourself again. To believe enough to actually start taking real life steps towards the change you know you need to make.

I want you to live out your full purpose and become exactly who God created you to be. I want you to stop looking at others who are living their lives with purpose with envy and start believing that you can be that person too, because you can!

> **Your Turn**
>
> What is the new script that you are going to tell yourself from now on when the lie that, "change only happens for others" comes into your head?

I Will Probably Fail

Oh the infamous "failure" that we all run and hide from. Why are we so afraid to fail? We believe that somehow our worth as a person is based on how many times we can avoid failure in our lives. It's like we are in this game where the person who fails the least in their life wins the biggest trophy.

Seriously, we avoid failure like the plague. By not stepping out and challenging ourselves we fool ourselves into thinking that we are strong because we are not failing. The truth is we are becoming weaker because we are letting fear hold us back.

Part of the reason we are afraid that we will fail is because we look at our struggle from the outside instead of the inside. Eleanor Roosevelt said it so eloquently, "No man is defeated without until he has first been defeated within." We look outward first and when we see how hard the challenge is we allow ourselves to become defeated on the inside.

You will fail many times in life, but that's when you take a deep breath and try again. Sometimes we are so afraid to fail that we won't even try unless we already know that we can succeed. This causes us to never venture outside of our comfort zones and test ourselves to see what we are really capable of. Fear prevents us from being our best.

When Thomas Edison was trying to invent the electric light bulb, he failed over 10,000 times. Imagine trying something 10,000 times, the patience and endurance it would take to not give up at time 100, let alone time 9,999.

The Five Non-Negotiables

When asked how he felt about failing that many times his response was, "I have not failed, I just found 10,000 ways that didn't work."

He understood that failure is part of the process of innovation and if you want to reinvent yourself you must have the same understanding.

You need to come to terms right now with the fact that you are going to fail. But failure is not a destination, it is a short stop along the way. Become comfortable with stepping out and failing. In the words of Vincent Norman Pearle, "Reach for the moon and if you fail you will land among the stars."

During the process of writing this book I have failed so many times at my non-negotiables. In fact I have failed at this so many times that I am a bit embarrassed to publish a book on something I have failed at so many times.

Even now, when I am almost done with this book which has been a several year journey to complete, I am still struggling and failing many times. I can tell you though that every time I fail I learn a new lesson about myself. I realize a wrong mindset I had, a habit I didn't realize was holding me back, or an excuse I didn't recognize was still lingering in my mind.

I can also tell you that I might not be anywhere near perfect at my non-negotiables, but I am light years ahead of when I started. I just keep getting back up every time I fall and I keep running my race. I never want to go back to the person I was before I started making these changes in my life.

So each time I fail, I learn. Each time I learn I get to come back to my non-negotiables stronger, wiser and better equipped than I was before. So perhaps I am a bit like Thomas Edison in that I am a good person to write this book not because I am perfect at the non-negotiables, but because I have failed 10,000 times, so hopefully I can help you avoid some failure in your own journey. Hopefully some of my failures will be lessons you can learn through my failures rather than your own.

Your Turn

What area of your life are you the most afraid to fail?

What have you avoided doing or putting your whole heart into doing because you are afraid you might fail or not be good enough at it?

What are you going to do about this fear of failure? Are you going to face it head on and pursue your answer above or are you going to let fear hold you back? This isn't a casual question, I am asking you to make a decision right now. Are you going to continue to let this fear of failure in this area hold you back, or are you going to face this fear and do something about it?

If you plan on confronting your fear and not letting it hold you back anymore, then what is the first step you are going to take towards accomplishing this?

I Will Start Tomorrow

The problem with starting tomorrow is that most often tomorrow never comes. The right time to start is right now. You didn't buy this book and take the time to read it to never actually start making the changes in your life. You bought this book because you decided that you are ready to actually make changes in your life.

You don't want to have regrets at the end of your life. Do not put off for tomorrow what can be done today. Get started right now!

That is why I have left you the space in the middle of the chapters to start writing down your goals and thoughts immediately, because if you wait till later, there is a good chance that later will never come. If you are waiting for the stars to all align and everything to be perfect to get started then you will never start.

Start now in the midst of the chaos. Start now when the odds are stacked against you. Start now when you are the underdog. Start now when you don't know the next step. Some of the greatest dreams have been accomplished when it seemed impossible. Start NOW! Like literally right now!

Your Turn

Turn back to page 35 and reread what you wrote about how you are committed to finally start making these life changes and why you are ready now.

Write "I am fully committed" below once you have completed this.

My Past Determines My Future

Everyone has a past riddled with mistakes and regrets yet when it comes to our own life for some reason we think our past is too horrible to permit us to have a great future. Everyone else is allowed to have a regretful or unqualifying past and still accomplish their dreams, but when it comes to ourselves, we think our past disqualifies us.

It is bad enough that we had to live through the misery in the past, but now we are willing to let it affect our futures too. No thank you! So you have a crappy past, you made some mistakes, you were born on the wrong side of the tracks, you didn't go to the "right" schools or you spent years in depression. You don't have the right connections, you got pregnant way too young, you had a debilitating addiction, you fell off the wagon for a while and lived a life that you now regret.

So freaking what. We all have a past. Trust me, there are many things in my past that I am not proud of. There are many dreams that I have in my heart that I am not technically "qualified" to fulfill. Dreams that will cost me money that I don't currently have, dreams that require training that I don't have. Dreams that require connections I don't have and skills that I have no experience in. Dreams that most people start at a younger age, but I am just starting now.

I love the stories of people who rose from a rough upbringing to become CEOs of major corporations or people who had drug addictions they overcame and ended up being all star professional athletes. The stories of the single moms who got pregnant at sixteen who have successfully started transitional homes for young moms who are going through what they overcame.

Those are the best stories, those are the stories that inspire us. The problem with these stories is that we see them as just that, a story. We don't see them as real life and we most certainly can't see them as a real life possibility for ourselves.

These are not just stories though, these are real people. People with real regrets and obstacles and fears. People who didn't always do everything right, people who took the road less traveled, had a few detours and had to do things the unconventional way.

People who are just like me and you. Our past is no predictor of our future. We create our own futures, we build our own lives. You are not limited because of your upbringing, you are only limited by yourself. So stop using your past as an excuse.

Stop living in the past. It is over. It is time to move on.

Your Turn

What is something in your past that you feel disqualifies you or is holding you back from living out your purpose fully?

If your friends told you they had made the same mistake in their past as you just wrote about so therefore they could never have a good future, what would you tell them?

Do you see the error in your original logic that your past disqualifies you? If you can write an argument to your friend, then you can write the same arguments to yourself. Write, "My past won't hold me back any longer, instead it will become my stepping stone towards my future" below.

What Will Others Think?

People's opinions, ugh... how we struggle so much with this one because we are looking for others to tell us who we really are. Will other's approve of my dream? What will my friends think? Will my husband think I am crazy? Will my parents disapprove?

Allowing yourself to ask these questions takes all the power of fulfilling your dream out of your own hands and places it into the hands of other people.

Don't even let the question of, "What will others think?" creep into your mind. It doesn't matter what others think, it's not their life it's your life. Don't let others determine what you can and cannot do in life based on what others will and will not approve of.

Don't waste one second of your valuable time and energy seeking to please others with your life. It is a futile effort. For one, you will never be able to succeed at pleasing everyone. Secondly, you will completely lose yourself in the pursuit of making others happy or impressed.

You cannot chase the approval of others and your dreams at the same time so make up your mind right now. Are you going to keep asking yourself will others approve? Or are you going to finally let others' opinions go and create your own life for yourself? Are you going to find the courage to pursue your dreams even if it means standing alone in your journey?

Your Turn

Who's opinion are you struggling the most to let go of? Your parents, spouse, friends, co-workers?

Why are you struggling with worrying about their opinion?

Are you going to let go of the worry of their opinion or are you going to continue to let their opinion hold you back? Why?

What would happen if you no longer asked the question, "what will others think?" What would your life look like?

Let's Be Real Honest Right Now

To be honest I feel like a complete hypocrite writing this chapter on excuses because I have struggled with almost every single one of these excuses. I am struggling big time with fear right now. In fact I am sitting on my closet floor at 5 AM writing this chapter because I could not sleep and this was the only place I could find to type that wouldn't wake up anyone else in my house. The reason that I am awake at 5 AM... my mind woke me up racing with fears and anxiety over this book.

Fear that I will write this entire book only to find out that no one wants to read it, or that once it is published people will hate it or judge me for it. I have struggled to stay motivated to keep writing day after day. I have second guessed myself a million times during this process wondering if this is a bad idea, or if I actually have anything important to say.

My most recent struggle has been being afraid of what people will think about me and this book once they have read it. My Christian friends will judge me because my book is too much about "works" and my non-Christian friends will judge me for talking about God. Everyone will judge me once they hear about my journey with depression like those mom's who judged me when I called them for advice when I was struggling.

I am afraid to fail at my dream of being an author. Most days when I work on this book I struggle with the feeling that maybe I am not really an author and I just made this idea up in my mind. I have no training or education in writing a book so I struggle with feeling qualified.

This dream is hard and scary. It has taken more discipline and commitment than I feel like I am capable of. Putting your voice and opinions out there in written form for all to scrutinize, analyze and have their own opinion about is terrifying.

Writing a book has been a dream in my heart since I was ten years old, but for some reason when it comes to actually trying to make this dream a reality, I feel so insecure.

I started writing this book scared, with no knowledge of how to write a book. I started without knowing everything I wanted to say or how to even correctly spell the word "definitely." When I started I didn't even honestly know much about how to stop negotiating with my own dreams.

In fact when I started this book all my life's dreams had been on the back burner for years. I had recently come out of a deep season of depression, I was not working out regularly, I was spending three hours a night binge watching TV, I was in survival mode with raising my kids and keeping the house in order.

Why am I telling you this? I want to be real with you right now in this moment while I too am in the middle of pursuing a dream and let you have a peek inside to my own reality of trying to make this book happen. I hope that by seeing my imperfect and real struggle, that you will gain hope that you can reach your dream.

I don't want you to only hear my testimony after my goal of publishing this book has been reached. I want to let you into the internal struggle that I am going through during the process of achieving my goal. Hopefully you can see a little bit of you inside of me and realize that we aren't so different and that will give you some hope to believe that you can do it too.

I also want you to see that there really are no good excuses to neglect your dream. Starting when you are unqualified, riddled with past failures, out of shape, unhappy and poor is totally fine. In fact I encourage it. Get started right now with what you have and as you use what you have it will grow.

It is so easy to look at people once they have accomplished their dreams and see an almost larger than life, super-hero type person and think, *I could never be as amazing as them*. I want to give you a real glimpse into the process of achieving your goal.

I want to share with you the middle of the process so that when you get to the middle and you start having doubts and fears you know that it is OK. That is a normal part of the process. It is ok to struggle, fail, start over, be insecure. All those things are fine as long as you still do it afraid, get up and try again when you fail and do it anyway.

One of the best parts about achieving your goal that hardly ever gets talked about is who you become in the process. It takes greatness to achieve your goals and that is who you become on the inside when you don't give up. Who you become during the process of pursuing your dreams is going to become so much more valuable than the dream itself.

The person you look up to who seems so great didn't start out that way. They had to make the same journey we all need to make in order to live out our purpose. They had to do it afraid, stop negotiating with themselves and commit. Do the hard things and overcome insecurities.

I started this journey of writing this book to help change other people's lives and the truth is that it ended up changing my life. The discipline that I have developed to sit at the computer day after day, the patience I have grown through the editing process and the courage I have had to build to let go of my fear of others opinions and to share my voice by publishing this is 100% worth the journey.

So stop making excuses and start doing the things that you know you should be doing. An amazing life is waiting for you on the other side of your excuses.

Non-Negotiable #4

Family

16

Non-Negotiable #4: Family

"If you want to bring happiness to the world, go home and love your family."

-Mother Teresa

How do you spell love? T-I-M-E!!! The truth is that we need to make time for the people we love.

I know this can be hard with our busy schedules. Balancing work, dropping the kids off at multiple schools each morning and then doing the carpool round up from school to school every afternoon. Fitting in homework and soccer practice and karate. The list of demands on us are endless.

There will always be a giant list of things to do, but if you spend your entire life waiting for those things to go away so you finally have time to spend with your spouse or kids, then you are going to miss your family.

Here is my question for you: Is your life passing you by and you can't seem to find the quality time you want and need for your spouse and kids?

This question is not meant to evoke the standard parent/spouse guilt, this is a sincere question that only you can answer for your family. I am not asking you if you are the perfect spouse or the perfect parent. I am asking you if you are spending the amount of time that you need with your spouse and kids? Don't compare yourself to other people that you know, take inventory of your own schedule and be honest with yourself.

Your Turn

Are you spending the amount of time and quality of time that you desire with your spouse?

Are you spending the amount of time and quality time that you desire with your kids?

Marriage

Why We Need To Prioritize Our Marriage

Life can get in the way of marriage very easily if we let it. One of the leading causes of marital problems is married couples putting their relationship on the back burner. I believe this because I have seen my own marriage struggle due in part to this exact issue.

My husband Michael and I are two strong and independent people. We are both go-getters with huge dreams. When we had kids we bought into the lies that the world around us kept telling us. Which included:

- Michael needs to put all his energy and time into his job so he can build his career. Once his career takes off, we will finally have time together and money to go on dates.
- Our kids are priority number one in our lives. Give them all your time and energy and once they are grown you will have time to reconnect with your spouse again.

The world told us a story of how we should live our lives and we bought into it hook, line and sinker. Everyone around us was doing all the same things: commuting hours to work each day, struggling to pay the bills, overwhelmed with debt and putting almost all their time and energy into their children and all their children's activities.

Everyone was overworked, over tired, close to burn out, but somehow they kept on going so we felt like we should too. We figured that was just the way life was supposed to be until the kid's grew up. We kept thinking that if we put all of our focus on our kids and Michael's job to pay the bills, then we would be just fine and after the kids were grown we could have more time for each other.

In fact there were times that I think I convinced myself that I was doing the right thing by neglecting my marriage in this season of raising small kids. All my energy went into the kids and the house leaving me with practically nothing for my husband at the end of the day.

We never spent any money on "us." Date nights, babysitters, gifts for each other were out of the question. But we would buy gifts for our children, make sure they had the best schools and tutoring help that they needed.

While it seemed like we were doing the "responsible" thing and even at times the "right" thing, I now look back and can see why our marriage struggled so much in certain seasons.

Although there are many other factors for marital problems, I am simply stating that if you don't make time for each other you are setting yourself up to fail. Disconnection and a lack of communication are common reasons for divorce. It is so easy to let the pressures around us begin to mold us and shape our schedules, instead of us taking control of our own schedules.

If you have been married for a while then you may have experienced a feeling of growing apart, lack of intimacy both physically and emotionally, a feeling of loneliness, a feeling that you are more roommates than spouses. You might have struggled with feeling unheard, unloved or unappreciated.

You may have felt any of these emotions from time to time because marriage is hard. It is two imperfect people pledging their lives together forever. In order to succeed at marriage and not just survive it, it takes hard work, sacrifice and making each other a priority.

Good Intentions

If you think about your life, besides your relationship with God and your relationship with yourself, your marriage is your most important and impactful relationship. If our marriage relationship is so important, then why do we put it on the back burner so often?

Many times our intentions are actually good: to help our kids, volunteer at the food bank, work extra hours to earn a pay raise, but we don't look at the big picture and realize all these "good intentions" are crowding out our most important intentions — having a great marriage.

Making time for your marriage is important. I hope you don't have to learn the hard way like I did. That is why setting aside the necessary time for your family is one of The Five Non-Negotiables. You don't want to look at your spouse in ten years and feel like you are looking at the face of a stranger.

Your marriage is meant to enrich your life, but the only way it will do so is if you invest in it. If you realize that life has crowded out some of the valuable time you should be investing in your spouse then now is a good time to stop and negotiate a new deal.

A healthy marriage affects your entire life, your spouse's entire life and your kids' lives. It is worth investing in.

Your Turn

Do you have some good intentions in your life that you now realize are taking away from your marriage?

What are the main things that are stealing time or energy and focus away from your marriage?

How To Prioritize Your Marriage

Michael and I lived this crazy fast paced life of "duty" for years until one day I had enough. I told Michael, "I am not living like this anymore. I miss you, I miss us. I miss having time together. I want to make a change."

Honestly it was hard to admit that I was unhappy at the time because I felt like admitting that I wasn't happy in this crazy life meant that I was weak and needy. It meant that I wasn't ok being like everyone around me and somehow that made me feel weak. Others before me have powered through this crazy life, so why can't I?

But the aching was just too big and the weariness was too much and I finally decided I didn't care about looking weak anymore. I wanted to finally be true to myself. I wanted to be my authentic self and that authentic self was tired and lonely and stressed.

We were growing apart and the only way to change that was for us to make a decision to change our priorities. We couldn't keep doing the same things we had been doing for years and expect our marriage to automatically become a priority just because we wanted it to be. We had to make some tough choices and cut things out to create time and space for each other again.

Sitting around feeling guilty, angry or disappointed that our marriage wasn't where we wanted it to be wasn't going to do us any good. We had to take action if we wanted our marriage to improve.

After years of living with jam packed schedules and a mindset that was all about the kids and growing Michael's career, it wasn't easy to make these changes. We were both set in our ways.

Thankfully Michael agreed with me that something needed to change and we started taking action together. We wanted to live closer to Michael's work so he wouldn't have to keep commuting three hours a day. The problem was that it was very expensive to live near his office, hence the long commute.

Our only solution was to sell our big house and move into a tiny house less than a mile from his office. We had to sell a lot of our furniture because our new home couldn't fit most of it. We also had to move our kids to new schools and ask them to make new friends.

This was not an easy move, but we knew that we needed to have more time together and cutting out Michael's commute would automatically give us about three more hours per day with him.

We also started going on dates again. This meant cutting back on other expenses so we would have a little money for dates. These changes were scary and hard, but looking back now I am so grateful that we did them. Being able to give our kids more time with their dad and having more time with Michael has made a huge difference.

Many times the reasons that people give for why they can't do something is really just an excuse. We have so much more power over our lives than we give credit. If you are unhappy, you can make a change. You aren't as stuck as you think you are.

I am sharing about my marriage and the changes we had to make in hopes that it will inspire you to take action and make the changes your marriage needs. This is your life, this is your marriage. Make it what you want it to be.

Hopefully you won't have to make as extreme changes as we did, but if you aren't prioritizing your marriage then you need to find a way to start.

Maybe you just need to pause at night before bed and start giving your spouse goodnight kisses again or take a few minutes to connect in the morning with your coffee before you both head out for the day. You don't have to go as extreme as we did, but I am sure there is something you can do to refocus more attention and energy on your marriage.

Your Turn

Are there some changes that you need to make so that you can make your marriage more of a priority?

---

10 Ideas To Invest In Your Spouse

There are many things you can do as a couple to enrich your marriage. I have included a few ideas to help get you thinking, but the sky's the limit.

1. There are lots of ways to focus on your marriage that don't cost a dime. There is one thing that I do want to say about money though. Part of making your marriage a priority might include occasionally spending money.

   We are willing to spend hundreds of dollars on make-up, clothes, eating out, the latest gadgets and home décor and fancy coffee drinks, but then when it comes to paying for a babysitter so we can go on a date, spending money on a marriage retreat or books on marriage or marriage counseling all of a sudden we pull out the "we can't afford that" card.

I know that each of us is in a different place financially so I am not trying to make you feel bad if money is tight and you honestly cannot afford some of these things, I have been there myself so I understand. That is not what I am talking about, what I am talking about is spending frivolously on things that are far less important than our marriage.

It is easy to develop a mentality that you never spend money on yourself or your spouse or your relationship because everything else seems more important. Just be sure that they really are more important. Also, dates don't have to be expensive. Spending an hour together at a coffee shop can do just as much for your marriage as an expensive five course meal.

2. If your routine consists of putting the kids to bed and then turning on the television and vegging the rest of the night till you fall asleep (no judgements here, I have totally done this like a million nights in a row), then consider choosing one night a week where you wait an hour before you turn on the T.V. and instead do something together first. After you have had some quality time together that first hour, then you can resume the vegging and fall asleep to your favorite show, but now you have had some time to connect first.

3. Write a funny joke on a sticky note and leave it on their toothpaste so they see it in the morning and start their day with a laugh.

4. Eat dinner outside. There is something about a change of scenery that makes dinner seem more intimate. A bonus is that the kids usually end up just wanting to go play in the yard leaving you to actually have some alone time during dinner to chat with your spouse.

5. Try to sneak out of work and meet up for a lunch date.

6. Have lunch delivered to your spouse at home or work with a note from you.

7.   After dinner, put on the song you danced to at your wedding and dance together.

8.   Buy a bunch of sticky notes and write one quality that you love or appreciate about your spouse on each one and fill your bedroom walls with them.

When they get home from work they can walk the whole room and read each word that you wrote. My husband kept the sticky notes on the walls for days because he said he loved being surrounded by them.

9.   Send your spouse a nice email in the middle of the day.

10. If your spouse uses the same products every morning to get ready, like toothpaste, hair gel, etc... Set it all out for them in the morning with a little love note.

My point in all of this rambling and list making is this: if your marriage is not a non-negotiable priority in your life right now, then stop in your tracks. Don't keep living life the same way and telling yourself things are going to change. Do something about it!

Your Turn

OK, I shared some of my fun ideas with you, now write down one thing you would like to do for your spouse this week. It doesn't have to be any of my ideas, do whatever you think will show your spouse how much you love them the most.

Now get out your calendar and schedule it in. Once you have set an exact time and day write, "My marriage is a priority" below.

I Don't Feel Like It

Perhaps you have gone on empty in your marriage for so long that you don't even know if it is worth the effort anymore. Maybe your marriage is at a hard place that is really suffering right now. You might be angry at or feel isolated from your spouse.

When you first get started reprioritizing your marriage you might not "feel" like doing it. It might simply be a "choice" that you are making. That is not easy, but it is worth it.

Learning to choose love even when you don't feel it, is to know what real love is. It is real love that has the power to change hearts and lives.

I know some of you are thinking, that sounds great, but my spouse will never change. I am willing to make our marriage a priority, but they are not. I am definitely no marriage counselor, but I would highly recommend you see a good one.

Sometimes we have to take the first step towards positive change and if we are consistent and non-negotiable in the changes, the people around us like what they see and decide they want to make changes as well. Leading by example can be extremely powerful.

Your Turn

Is your marriage a non-negotiable priority? I am not asking if you have the perfect marriage, I am asking you if you are giving the right amount of effort and priority to your marriage. I do not want you to take this time to start beating yourself up if you're not prioritizing your marriage. Everyone struggles with prioritizing their marriage so don't feel bad about it. Instead, if you know you and your spouse need more quality time together then be proactive and start scheduling it in.

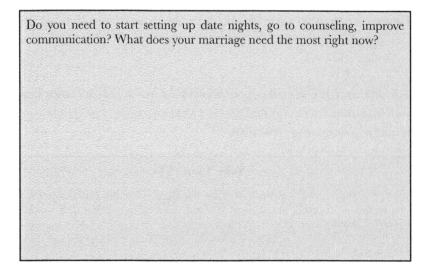

Do you need to start setting up date nights, go to counseling, improve communication? What does your marriage need the most right now?

It Is Worth It

I am so grateful that Michael and I made the changes necessary to begin to prioritize "us." I am not saying we have the perfect marriage or that we always get our date time in. We are far from all that, we still have struggles and disagreements and stress and life constantly trying to crowd each other out.

We are still learning how to grow our marriage and connect on deeper levels, but we have come a long way in prioritizing each other and spending quality time together and my heart is full.

My husband's current schedule has him starting his days later which also means they end later, so we switched up our dinner dates to breakfast dates. On date days, we drop the kids off at school and go to breakfast together before we start our day.

No matter how much our schedules change, we are committed to making time together and because of that we are more connected now than we have ever been in any other season of our marriage. I thought I loved Michael the day I married him, but I have grown to love him so much more than I ever knew was possible.

For those of you who are married or have been married, you know what a blessing a healthy marriage can be. Good marriages don't just happen though, they take work.

Your marriage is one of the more important parts of your life, treat it as such by making it a priority and it will be a blessing to you. I promise you investing in your marriage is worth it.

Your Turn

Write about a sweet season in your marriage. A time when you felt connected and loved. What were you and your spouse doing that made you feel loved?

Wedding Advice

Before we got married Michael and I received lots of advice including, "Be sure to make each other a priority." "Don't forget to have date nights and do things to keep the love alive." I heard their words, but for some reason I totally forgot to apply them.

Maybe I was arrogant and assumed that nothing could ever break our marriage and we didn't need to worry about the worries of the world creeping in and creating space. Perhaps I was just so caught up in being "in love" and assumed life would always be this way and no stress, job or kids could come between what I was feeling at that moment. Either way, the bottom line is that I didn't choose to live out that wise and sound advice and my marriage paid the consequences of such.

My prayer is not for you to simply read this, it is for you to live it. To stop missing out on having a full heart and a spouse that makes you feel loved and appreciated because your priorities are out of order.

When you plan out your week you should be thinking about more than just your to-do's, you should also be thinking about your "who's." Who do you need to be scheduling into your calendar this week? Your spouse should always be at the top of that list. If you want to make sure something gets done because it is important to you, then you usually write it down in your calendar and schedule it in. It is no different with your spouse.

Your Turn

Do you have regular time scheduled to connect with your spouse? If not then this needs to become a non-negotiable in your life. From this point on, your marriage needs to become a priority.

Talk this over with your spouse and come to an agreement for a mutual goal that you will share to spend quality time together. Are you going to have a date night once a week, a getaway once a month? Make this goal specific to your marriage, the only stipulation is that you are consistent.

Once you have talked this over with your spouse and set your goal, write it here.

Write out why you are going to make these dates happen. Why is it important to you to connect with your spouse regularly? Why is your marriage important to you?

Pull out your calendar and schedule in your regular "date" time. Then write "I'm going on a hot date" here once you have completed this.

Just like you have with all your other non-negotiables, add your marriage goal and why into your list to review each day. When the alarm goes off in the morning this will be what your review daily to help keep you on track. Write" I love my spouse" below once you have completed this.

Kids

Parent Guilt

We basically have about 6,600 days with our kids from birth until they become adults. It might sound like a lot of time, but those 6,600 days fly by quickly.

When our kids are born we promise ourselves that we will spend lots of time with them and we mean it. Then as time goes on and life creeps in, many of us end up feeling like we just don't have the time that we had hoped.

Life seems to have an endless list of demands that are stealing away the time and energy that we would rather be spending with our kids. Then, when we see other parents that look like they are spending way more time with their kids than us the parent guilt starts creeping in.

As we compare ourselves to other parents or against some of our naive unrealistic parenting expectations we set for ourselves we begin to feel horrible. We tell ourselves that we aren't good parents or that our kids are going to have issues because we didn't play at the park with them enough.

We are really good at beating ourselves up. The problem is that the guilt is not doing you any good. When you feel guilty about something, but you never do anything about it, you stay in a constant state of guilt that eats away at you.

Do You Get Enough Time With Your Kids?

Most parents feel guilty about not spending enough time with their kids. The question I want to ask you here is, do you personally get enough quality time with your kids? Do you need more time with your kids or do you have enough time with them, but you still feel guilty because of comparison or unrealistic expectations?

I am not asking you to compare with how much time you think other parents get with their kids. I don't want you to base your answer on some imaginary unrealistic "perfect parent" standard that you try to hold yourself to. I am also not asking you if you are spending the exact amount of time that you ideally would get to spend with your kids in a perfect world.

None of those things matter. Those ideas won't allow you to honestly evaluate your life based on your unique situation, children and schedule. The amount of quality time necessary for each parent and child will be different. There is no specific standard I am trying to hold you to other than what you feel is best for you and your children.

The quality of time you get with your kids is so much more important than the quantity. I know SAHM's who feel guilty about not spending enough time with their kids and I know working moms who feel they do get enough time with their kids.

I know that after years of beating yourself up with parent guilt it can be hard to even know how to have realistic expectations and answer this question honestly. I want you to dig deep. Examine your relationship with each of your kids and honestly ask yourself if you feel you are able to invest in each of them in the way that you both need to have a healthy relationship.

It's ok to evaluate an area of your life and come to the conclusion that you aren't hitting the mark you want to be hitting. No one is hitting the mark in every area of their life, that's just not realistic. When you can be secure enough in yourself to allow yourself to be honest, that is when you can find the truth.

Once you know the truth, you can make a game plan to change your situation.

Your Turn

Do you feel like you do need to carve out more time for your kids? Or do you think you have been living under an unrealistic expectation for the amount of time you should be spending with your kids and feeling guilty for falling short in an area that you are actually doing just fine in?

How To Make More Time

If you aren't getting enough time with your kids then let's talk about it.

Do you need to cut some things out to make more time for them, or are you like me with crazy unrealistic expectations of parenthood that will always leave you in a pile of guilt because no matter what you can never live up to them.

Whichever it is, it's time to stop living in guilt and time to start making some changes.

If you feel like your relationship with your kids could use a little more time and energy, then let's see where you can carve it out. Let's do something to make a change and not just sit around feeling guilty about it.

Below are a few ideas I put together of things that might be stealing some of the time you would probably rather be investing in your kids.

Busyness

Life is so over scheduled that we just don't have the time or energy to have quality time with our kids. Running from event, to activity, to task all day long everyday leaves us no time for real connection.

I am a mom, but my title should also include chauffeur, maid, chef, personal secretary, nurse, teacher, among many other things. Most of my days are filled with things I need to do for my kids. It can be so easy to get caught up in doing for our kids that we forget to make time to spend with our kids.

Look at your to-do list, is there a small task that you could push over till tomorrow and instead spend those few minutes with your child? Those few extra minutes that can make a big difference.

Television

When we are busy and stressed out it can be so much easier to turn on the TV and let everyone spend time with the show rather than with each other. There is absolutely nothing wrong with watching TV, we love our family movie nights!

But when every single free minute of downtime is watching TV or playing video games, you might be missing out on some precious time that you could be playing a game together or having great conversations.

I don't think we always realize how much of our time or our kids' time really does go to watching TV. Stealing just a small portion of that TV time to spend with our kids can make a big difference in our relationship with them.

Phones

It is so easy to get into the habit of pulling out our phone every time we have a few free minutes. At one point I was so addicted to my phone that I was literally pulling it out whenever I was at a red light because I couldn't handle waiting two minutes at a stop light without being entertained.

I refused to look at my phone while driving, but whenever I was at a stop light I would pull it out. Every time I was waiting in line at the grocery store or waiting for my tea order at the coffee shop I would completely ignore everyone around me and pull my phone out.

When you are alone that's not a big deal (well looking at your phone at red lights isn't good), but when you are with your kids you are losing precious moments to connect with them.

Before we had cell phones, and more specifically social media, we used to spend those moments engaging with the people who were with us or other people around us. Now it is almost like we use our phones as an excuse to be anti-social.

It is so easy to look at our phones every time we have a free moment instead of engaging with our kids. I catch myself doing this at times. Jordyan or Reese will be trying to talk to me and I am busy reading someone's Facebook post and not paying attention to them. Let's make sure our phones aren't stealing precious time away from our kids.

Take Advantage Of Little Moments

You don't necessarily have to spend a lot of time every single day. Some-times it is just about taking advantage of the little moments you have to-gether.

Trying to spark up a good conversation while you are driving to baseball practice or spending time playing tic-tac-toe while you are waiting for your doctor's appointment. Stealing away little moments throughout the day allows you to constantly be connected with your child without feeling the burden of needing to set aside two whole hours just to play with them when you have deadlines at work.

Get good at recognizing those little moments together and use them as opportunities to bond with your child.

Real Life Superhero

I want to start this section with a Your Turn, you get to start and I will go second :)

Your Turn

Think about your superhero, the person that you really really look up to. It can be a famous singer or painter, an actual superhero or movie character, maybe a CEO or business leader or a person from history. Who is the one person that you look up to the very most? Write their name here.

Ok, now imagine that this person boards a plane and flies down to your house just to have lunch with you. They put their phone away and all distractions and spend time with you for an hour straight. How would that make you feel? Write it out in detail below.

You have basically just described how your child feels when you unplug from everything around you and spend quality time with them. You are your kids' real life superhero. While we might not have super powers, we do have a lot of power to love and influence our children. As Winston Churchill said, "With great power comes great responsibility."

We are responsible for prioritizing our children. We need to make time to connect with each of our children consistently. Unfortunately this doesn't always happen naturally, we have to actually plan for it and we have to be intentional.

I am the first to admit that spending quality time with my children can be inconvenient. I know that probably makes me sound like a horrible mother, but it is true. I have a busy life and setting time aside to play dolls on the floor or build a fort in the backyard doesn't exactly help me get my daily tasks accomplished.

Dropping everything and giving my kids my undivided attention by having a tea party for the millionth time can be a sacrifice. It can mean staying up later to finish my work or not getting my grocery shopping done that day, but quality time is not just a good idea, it is literally a prerequisite for a good relationship with your child.

Ideas For Quality Time

Below I have included some ideas of things I have done to spend quality time with my kids. I am sure that you can add to this list or come up with even better ideas than mine, this is just a short list to get you started.

1. Go out for ice cream or in my case Kombucha. My daughter and I share an affinity for Kombucha and I found a little Kombucha bar in town that sells specialty Kombuchas and it is our secret place that just the two of us go to for dates. If you have no idea what Kombucha is then you are seriously missing out!

2. Go through a devotional book together. My daughter and I are currently going through a great devotional for pre-teens. It is called "Can You Relate?" by Vicki Courtney. It talks about boys, mean girls and how to deal with them, how to grow close to God at their

age and so much more. It also includes quizzes and games for them to do which makes it really fun and interactive.

3. Go in your kid's room and join in on whatever they are doing: playing Legos, drawing a picture, etc... ask to join in and soak in the quality time with them doing something they love to do. Reese loves it when I randomly come in while she is playing Legos and start building with her.

4. Sometimes I build a little makeshift fort with blankets and chairs in my living room floor or in the backyard and then I invite one of them to join me to "hang out" or we will have dinner in the "secret hideout" that night. The girls love it, I don't know what it is about being in a tent, but it makes dinner so much more fun and gets the girls chatting about their day and really focusing on "us."

5. Occasionally I will tell them in advance that I am taking them on a date in a couple days and ask them to choose where they want to go. The anticipation for them is so exciting and they feel so special when they get to be on a date with one of their parents.

6. Wake up early on a school day and surprise the kids with a trip to the park before school. My kids love this. Spending the morning outdoors rejuvenates the mind and soul. Also, you usually get the entire park to yourselves because there are not many other crazy moms out there that are taking their kids to the park at 6:30 AM on a Wednesday. You can even have a "breakfast picnic" while you are there.

   I started taking them to the park in the morning before school on rainy days because Reese was complaining that on rainy days she didn't get to have an outdoor recess. I told her that I could fix that and we drove to the park before school and had recess in the rain. Yes I did drop them off at school wet and muddy and I am sure their teachers thought we were crazy, but they had the best time.

7. Have lunch with them at school. My kids love it when I surprise them and show up at their school with food from their favorite restaurant. They get a break from those PB&J sandwiches and I get to spend time with them in their world.

I also get to know their friends really well by doing this. My daughters proudly give me a tour of the entire playground and introduce me to all of their friends.

8. Have a date jar. This is a jar full of fun date activities. These could include: having a tea party, going to the park or throwing the football together. You can include as many fun ideas for mini-dates in the jar as you want and at the beginning of the month you can have each kid draw one idea out of the jar and you guys book a time that month to go and do it together.

9. Face painting. My kids love to do face paint. There is something about being close enough to paint each other's faces that makes them open up. I usually paint their faces and then they paint mine together.

   Each child gets to paint one half of my face so you can imagine how I end up looking. One side is a dog and the other is a butterfly. The entire time they are painting away they will talk and talk and I learn so much about them. Doing any activity that makes them feel like you are coming down to their level and being a kid with them can make them feel so excited and special.

There are a million ideas out there, I just wanted to share a few to get you thinking. What if you planned just two activities a month to do with your kids? I don't know how many kids you have or how busy your schedule is, but if you could fit in a little date time with each child or even all together with the children at the same time it will grow your relationship with them.

It will allow them to have your undivided attention in a fun setting where work and stress and bills are not welcome. Only fun and love and listening are allowed.

You don't have to change your entire life around to have quality time with your kids. You just need to be purposeful about it and schedule it to make sure it happens.

Don't Get Overwhelmed

I want to take a minute here to remind you that you don't have to do all five non-negotiables at once. My goal is not to overwhelm you, but to help you start taking baby steps in prioritizing the most important things in your life.

If you have already set a goal for another non-negotiable and you aren't ready to take on an additional goal yet, that is just fine. You can continue to read the book while working on your first goal.

You don't have to set a goal with every non-negotiable all at once to make progress. Improving in one area at a time is perfectly fine. Don't stop reading though, because each chapter is designed to help you take consistent action in your goals. As you read you will continue to gain tips, tools and motivation to help you with whatever non-negotiable goal you are working on at this time.

Your Turn

Write the names of your kids below.

Now write down a few things that you could do to spend quality time with each of them. Choose things that you think that particular child would like best. If Tiffany likes to get dressed up maybe she would like a fancy tea party. If Ethan likes building, maybe he would enjoy some Lego time with you. Be specific for each individual child.

Now set a non-negotiable goal for spending quality time with your kids. It can be once a week, once a month, whatever works for you and your family, but make a commitment that is consistent to set aside quality time with each child. It doesn't have to be long, but it has to be consistent. Write your goal below. If you don't want to set a goal for "date" time with your kids then maybe you just want to set a goal to spend less time on your phone when they are around. You can set any goal that you want.

Use this space to write your why. Why are you going to start being intentional about spending time with your kids? Why is this important to you? Why is this important to them?

You already know what I am going to ask you to do next, pull out your calendar again. Schedule in each one of your quality time dates. If you don't have "dates" as your goal then schedule in whatever it is that your goal is. Write, "I am not going to feel parent guilt anymore, instead I am going to schedule time with my kids when I can and let go of guilt the times I can't." once you have scheduled it.

Setting aside specific quality time with your kids is now a non-negotiable. This means you need to add it to your list of goals that you review every morning when the alarm goes off. Add your goal and why now and write, "I love my kids and I can't wait to spend quality time with them" below once you have completed this.

Four Things You Need To Hear

1. <u>You are a good mom/dad.</u>

    I love the quote by Jill Churchill that says, "There is no way to be a perfect mother, and a million ways to be a good one." Don't beat yourself up, you're doing a good job at one of the hardest jobs in the world.

2. <u>You don't have to listen to every opinion.</u>

    My opinion of opinions is that most of them suck. Everyone is so quick to hand out their opinions on how others should be living their life or parenting their kids when no one even asked them.

    You have the right to completely ignore others' opinions (mine included). I am all about good solid advice that is helping, but unsolicited opinions are not welcome.

    Be yourself, trust yourself. Seek advice when you need it, but don't just accept an opinion because it was handed to you. You have the right to reject opinions that aren't right for you.

3. <u>It's ok to make mistakes and not have it all together.</u>

    When your children become parents are you going to expect that they are perfect and always have it all together? Are you going to be worried that your grandkids are going to grow up to be a complete mess because your kids weren't the perfect parent for them?

    Of course not. You would never expect perfect parenting from your own children, but for some reason you probably expect it from yourself.

    I usually do my best parenting when I am the least stressed out and in the most positive mindset. If we keep beating ourselves up every day over every little mistake we make then we will constantly be in a stressed and negative headspace. This will make us a lot more likely to make mistakes.

    Give yourself some grace and let go of the mistakes you make. Your child is going to be just fine.

4. <u>You are still you.</u>

    Yes you have become a parent and a lot has changed, but you are still yourself. Your roles have expanded, but who you are at the core has not.

    You don't need to ignore or suppress who you are just because you have become a parent. Once we have kids we tend to completely forget who we are as an individual.

    Don't ever feel bad about being just you and wanting just you to still have a voice or space in your life. You have not replaced who you are by having kids, you have simply added on to it.

One Last Thing

I want to reiterate one last time. The point of this chapter is not to make you feel guilty. It is to help you start taking baby steps towards change. The point of this chapter is that hopefully now that you have set a plan of action you can start doing the things you need to do and let go of the guilt in your family relationships.

My prayer is that this chapter has empowered you so that instead of still feeling guilty, in a year from now you can be proud of yourself and the progress you have made. Progress that has led you to an even closer and more fulfilling relationship with your kids and spouse.

My greatest desire for you is that your spouse, kids and your own life will be enriched because you took action. So many people spend their whole lives paralyzed by guilt or fear and never stop their busy lives for a minute to evaluate whether they are doing the whole marriage or parenting thing in a fruitful way for them.

You should be proud of yourself for taking this pause and being honest enough to evaluate your relationships and make course corrections where necessary.

17

Be Consistent

"Success is neither magical nor mysterious. Success is the natural consequence of consistently applying basic fundamentals."

-E. James Rohn

Consistency literally had to be one of my least favorite words on the planet. I felt the same way about consistency that the Grinch felt about Christmas. Do you remember in the movie *The Grinch* (played by Jim Carey) when referring to Christmas when he says, "I hate hate hate, double hate, loathe entirely"? That pretty much sums up the way I felt about consistency.

To me consistency felt like this unrealistic object that I was trying to obtain or an impossible mountain that I was trying to climb. I had a better chance at winning the lottery than I did at sticking with something for more than a week.

The Five Non-Negotiables

One thing I have learned about consistency though, is that you can hate it all you want, but without it you will never be all that you were born to be. I personally will never reach my goals, be the mother, wife, author and healthy person that deep inside I am born to be.

My brother, Justin, is obsessed with CrossFit, in fact he founded the largest CrossFit news outlet in the world called, "Morning Chalk Up." Being such a CrossFit enthusiast, my brother made me a challenge: He would pay for my CrossFit gym membership if I was willing to give it a try. The problem was I was out of shape.

I mean like the: I-have-pushed-out-two-babies-and-hardly-done-anything-in-years kind of out of shape. Money was tight for Michael and I though, so I figured this was probably my one and only chance to try and get back into shape so I hesitantly said yes.

I started attending classes right away. At first I was my usual inconsistent self, showing up to class four times in a row one week and the next week I wouldn't even go once. I was all over the place and I wasn't seeing any changes in my body or health so of course I started with the excuses.

"I don't really like CrossFit, the workouts are strange and I don't feel like this is working for me" I would whine. "I am too busy to go everyday." The list of my excuses would go on and on, but the truth was that I wasn't willing to be consistent.

I had all the ingredients to become healthy again. My kids were now in school during the day so I had the time to attend class, my brother was paying for my membership, so money was not an issue. I had all the right workout gear collecting dust in my closet. I even had the desire to get into shape. I mean what more could a girl ask for? I had more than I technically needed and yet somehow I still wasn't able to get in shape.

The only missing ingredient was my willingness to be consistent. Desire is not enough, you need to be committed and commitment equals consistency and consistency equals results.

I know what it is like to go through life feeling like you have so much more to give, but not having the discipline or consistency to bring those gifting's to full fruition. I know what it is like to be stuck in a sub-par life because I didn't have the drive to consistently pursue my goals. I know what it is like to settle for second best because I couldn't muster up the strength to make the hard choices I needed to make to be the best version of myself. I know what it is like to live life just going through the motions and to put it in layman's terms, it really sucks.

It sucks not being healthy, it sucks feeling like your money disappears into a dark, never-ending hole each month. It sucks feeling stressed all the time and having no work/life balance. It sucks knowing that there is so much more inside you and you aren't operating at your full potential. It sucks feeling an energy slump every day at noon and having high blood pressure that keeps you up at night.

It sucks feeling like you have nothing to give to others because you can't even take care of yourself. It sucks being depressed and unmotivated, being controlled by your cravings and emotions. I know these things suck because I have experienced most of them.

It is time to stop living such sucky lives!

Wake Up Call

Ring, Ring, Ring... this is your wake up call! Just like when you stay at a hotel and they call you in the morning to wake you up. I am calling you right now and saying IT'S TIME TO WAKE UP!!! It's time to wake up from your sleepy halfway living.

WAKE UP!!! Right here and right now, take your life back. Decide to be fully awake in your life, in your health, finances and family! WAKE UP!!! Why are you here? What is your purpose? What are you living for today? WAKE UP!!!

The Five Non-Negotiables

If you have been waiting for a sign from God then here you go... WAKE UP!

Think about your life for a minute. Are there areas where you have substituted consistency for excuses? If you were to honestly evaluate your life without excuses and pretense, you might recognize that you are just like me. With all the ingredients you need for success, but lacking in consistency.

We are so blessed in life and oftentimes we don't recognize it because our blessings are piled under a mound of excuses. We are sitting around waiting for that breakthrough or miracle to happen when all the while we have everything we need to go make our own miracle in our hands already.

To be honest, I didn't even technically need a gym to get back into shape. Of course going to a gym is great, but I could have gone running around my neighborhood. Trust me there are plenty of hills where I live to get my butt in shape. I didn't even need the fancy workout clothes, I could have worked out in my old shorts and t-shirts.

Can you relate to my story? Not just in the area of working out, but in your own life in other areas as well? Areas where you have all the ingredients for success, but somehow you still are not succeeding?

I look back at my life and can see so many things that I missed out on because I refused to show up consistently. Excuses are so much easier, but they also leave us at a place of personal compromise. We are capable of much more, but excuses allow us to settle.

Your Turn

Do you struggle with being consistent?

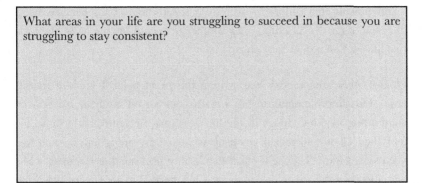

What areas in your life are you struggling to succeed in because you are struggling to stay consistent?

Becoming Consistent

The good news to this story is that I did eventually become consistent. I made a commitment to go to the gym four or five days a week no matter what. Attending CrossFit no longer became a negotiable issue in my life. I had a conversation with myself and I made a deal. I wrote out a contract and I signed it. I sealed the deal and there was no going back.

Within a few weeks of being consistent I started to improve. I chose to keep the agreement I made with myself. Trust me, all those old excuses tried to creep back into my mind, but I took my contract with myself seriously, like an important business contract. Because I am important and my word is not just my bond to others, it is my bond to myself. I deserve to be treated with respect and dignity and integrity. It was about time I started treating myself that way.

My brother had no idea at the time when he made his generous offer/ challenge the effect that it would have on my life. Before becoming committed to exercising I was much more of a wanderer. I had two beautiful girls whom I stayed home with and I loved being there for them every minute, but those of you who stay at home know that the life of a SAHM does nothing to help foster consistency. You can't even consistently take showers most days.

I had become a real expert at using the typical "mom excuses" to justify or give myself permission to be less than I was capable of being. Somehow finally making that commitment to exercise led me into another new habit of eating right which led me into another new habit of pursuing my goals that have sat on a shelf for years.

One of those major goals was writing this exact book. I know it sounds crazy, but simply committing to working out set off a chain reaction of committing to other things in my life. Working out consistently somehow took the lock off the door in my heart where all my strength to commit had been stored away. I thought I just didn't have it in me, but the truth was I had a lot more in me than I thought. I just needed to stick with something long enough to uncover it.

After joining CrossFit and actually becoming committed to something important to me, I have realized that I don't actually hate consistency. I just felt powerless to achieve it, therefore like a jealous girl in high school who hates the popular girl because she isn't popular herself, I chose to exude hate towards consistency.

I actually resisted it and made excuses saying, "Well doing that every day will make me feel boxed in", or "no one actually sticks to that", or "that just isn't realistic for my life", or my best one… "I just wasn't born a consistent person, it's just not a part of my personality."

Your Turn

What excuses do you use that keep you from being consistent?

Are these excuses helping you? What benefit are these excuses bringing to your life?

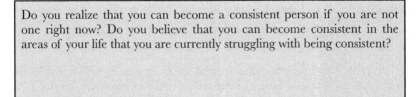

Do you realize that you can become a consistent person if you are not one right now? Do you believe that you can become consistent in the areas of your life that you are currently struggling with being consistent?

Consistency vs Emotions

It is true that some people are born with a personality that tends to be more consistent than others. It is also true that it is not just the people who have a bent towards consistency that need consistency in their lives. We all need consistency in order to be successful and reach our goals.

One of the best ways to be inconsistent is to live a life led by our emotions. I tell my kids all the time that feelings are meant to be followers and not leaders. If I am led by my feelings then I will eat whatever I feel like, whenever I feel like it. I will treat those around me based on the way they make me feel or what mood I am in at the moment. I will spend money whenever I feel like it regardless of whether I have the money or not. You get the picture.

Letting emotions lead our lives guarantees us a life of total inconsistency. It is easy to give into our emotions. They are strong and they are constantly fighting for our attention. Every time we let them lead our choices though they start us down a rabbit hole of destruction.

I don't know about you, but my emotions are like the weather in the midwest. It can snow, hail and be sunny all in the same day. When I lived in Oklahoma, I felt like I always needed a parka jacket and a t-shirt in the trunk of my car just to be prepared for the day. You could walk into a store with a t-shirt on since it was 95°F and walk out two hours later and it is 60°F with a wind chill of 50°F.

Likewise, I can be happy one minute, mad the next, thirty minutes later I am crying and by dinner time I can be happy again. I can't let this roller coaster of emotions be my compass each day. I need to gain control over these emotions and make my decisions based on my non-negotiables, my goals, and my purpose. I need to stay committed no matter how I feel.

For years of my life I had the bad habit of letting my emotions lead me. Until I finally got sick and tired of being in the same place, stopping and starting things over and over, making promises to myself that I never kept and feeling like I had no power to really affect change in my life because I didn't have the discipline to be consistent. My lack of consistency has robbed me of years of my life that I could have been so much healthier, better off financially and further along in my goals and dreams.

Your Turn

Do you let your emotions get in the way of being consistent? If so, what are the main emotions that tend to get in your way?

There may be regrets that you have from the past, now is the time to let them go. Holding onto your mistakes will weigh you down. Write down some of the regrets you have in relation to your goals.

Now is the time to forgive yourself and let go of your regrets. They are not serving you well so start focusing on who you are becoming and not who you were in the past.

Write yourself a forgiveness letter. Just as you would write to someone who had hurt you that you were forgiving. Write a letter of forgiveness to yourself for the years wasted, the stop and starts and the regrets. Write this letter from your heart and release yourself from the regret. Use this letter as an opportunity to let go of the past and start new.

You have a bright amazing future ahead of you, let's not take baggage from the past with us. Side note: Don't take the expectation of perfectionism with you into the future. Once you forgive your past, have a realistic expectation of the future. You want to learn to be consistent, but it is ok if you can't always be consistent. You need to be balanced.

Don't Quit When It Gets Hard

Still showing up when you are tired, the kids have worn you out, no one else believes in you, you doubt yourself, you are having a rough day... That is the hardest part.

"To show up or not to show up.... That is the question." OK so I am no Shakespeare, but you get the point. That really is the question, are you going to show up?

My old fitness coach taught us that we shouldn't give up when it gets hard during a workout, because it's when the workout gets difficult and you feel like quitting that is when most of your endurance and muscle growth happens.

The way you grow more muscle is to push your muscles to the point that they actually begin to make tiny micro tears in them. When these tears heal they grow back stronger and bigger than before.

When the weight gets heavy and you feel like you just can't lift it one more inch, that is when the real growth in your muscles happen. That is when the tiny muscle fibers begin to rip and tear to make room for bigger, stronger muscle fibers. But if you quit the moment it gets hard you will never get any stronger.

All the working out that you do before it gets hard is simply just to get you to the point of wanting to give up, because then, once you are at the point of hurting and wanting to quit, but you choose to keep on going anyways, that is where the most muscle growth happens. That is the "sweet spot." All the work you did before was to get you to that point.

The same applies in life, if you keep starting things and then quitting as soon as it gets painful or hard or inconvenient, you will never make it to that "sweet spot" that will propel you forward in growth. When it gets hard, the moments when you want to give up the most, those are the moments you must not quit. Those are your "sweet spots" and you don't want to do all that work and get to a moment of growth and end up giving up right before it happens.

Dig deep and embrace the pain, let yourself venture past your comfort zone and experience the "sweet spot." Trust me, that is where some of your best moments of growth and transformation will happen, the moments after you did it afraid, after you pushed yourself beyond the limits you previously had for yourself.

(Disclaimer: I am not telling anyone to go crazy at the gym and to never take breaks. I am not telling you to push yourself too hard nor am I telling you to workout when you have injuries and pain. I don't want to get any emails from people who are injured because they pushed themselves too hard in their workouts. That is not what I am promoting. Take breaks when you need to and listen to your body when you exercise. Be smart and only push yourself to a safe and healthy level and always consult a doctor before beginning a new exercise routine.)

Your Turn

When is a time that you pushed through the pain and kept going and you experienced a breakthrough or a giant leap forward in your life?

The Storms

I want to take a minute to talk about the times in life when we are going through really hard times. Sometimes in the midst of the storm one of the best things we can do is to stay consistent in what we know and ride it out. Sometimes our greatest weapon against the storm can be our consistency.

If you feel like you are in a storm right now, maybe life is crashing in on you at all sides and you feel that your boat is sinking. If you are on the brink of giving up or in the middle of a battle just keep showing up. I know that is not the comforting advice that you would like to hear, but just because your life has not turned out the way you anticipated, or you have made huge mistakes or you are in the middle of a struggle, it does not mean that you cannot reach your goals and dreams.

I want to tell you a little secret about storms. This is a secret I learned when I was deep down in my own storm of depression.

Storms don't have the ability to be consistent, they cannot last forever.

Storms can only last in one place for a while and then they must move on. But you my friend, you have the power to be consistent in the midst of the storm. You have the one trait that the storm does not, you can remain. A storm does not have the ability to outlast you if you choose to be consistent. Storms only get to stay for a while, but you are unmovable.

A storm might be tough and hard and intense, but it also has an expiration date. The saying is true, "a bright sunny day comes after the rain."

Your struggle is not the end of your story, your mistakes are not a death sentence to your dreams, but you must keep showing up every day in the midst of the storm. If no one else in life is showing up for you, then show up for yourself. Refuse to give up. When others doubt you, sing louder than their doubt, when fear tries to creep in, yell louder than the fear, when hard times come your way, be stronger than the hard times.

You are stronger than you know, much more resilient than you realize. If you want to reach your goals then you are going to have to learn to be consistent and outlast the storms and I know you can do it. This storm is not the end of your story, it is the beginning. Just keep showing up despite your feelings and I promise you, you will make progress.

Your Turn

Are you going through a storm right now? If so, write about it below.

Whether or not you are going through a storm, write out a note of encouragement to yourself that you can look back on to help you get through the storms in your life.

18

How To Stick With Your Goals Through Life's Interruptions

"Our greatest glory is not in never falling, but in rising every time we fall."

-Confucius

A few years back I made the decision to take my health seriously. I set goals and started working hard on them. I found a CrossFit gym that I loved and switched my food to healthier choices. The best part was... I was actually being consistent!

I was so excited about how healthy I was feeling, when one Friday evening I started having abdominal pain. Early the next morning I ended up in the emergency room and was hospitalized for over a week while they ran tests trying to figure out what was wrong with me. I was finally ushered into surgery.

The Five Non-Negotiables

When I came out of the surgery the doctors informed me that I would need a second surgery after I recovered from the first one. I was so disappointed. I had worked really hard and now I was being told I could not even step foot in a gym for at least six weeks, no lifting weights for ten weeks and once I was fully recovered I was going to have to do it all over again for my second surgery.

In total, it was about a five month set back in my goals. All of the progress that I had made prior to these surgeries was lost and my stomach was the weakest it had ever been.

Has this ever happened to you?

You are on track working hard to achieve your goals and stay on routine when out of nowhere something happens that completely messes up your schedule. The kids get sick, work gets busy, the holiday season, etc... Life just keeps getting in the way.

I call this getting derailed. Just like a train headed to its destination when suddenly one of the tracks comes loose and the train falls off the rails.

Life is not an uninterrupted train ride from destination to destination. It is full of many twists and turns. Everyday we face unexpected circumstances that can derail us from our goals.

Your Turn

What are some of your goals that you would like to achieve, but you constantly feel like you're getting derailed in?

What are the top three things that keep derailing you? (Work dinners, lack of preparation, holidays).

Don't Use The Derailment As An Excuse

So how do we ever achieve anything if we keep getting derailed? Here are a few lessons I have learned along the way that have helped me get back on track quickly.

Your kid gets sick and you can't work on your business that day. That is just the way life is sometimes. But when your child is better and back to school you need to get right back at your business. No excuses, no delays.

Once we get derailed it is easy to make excuses to stay off track. "Well just one more day and then I will get back at it" or "It's almost the weekend so there is no point in starting back today, I'll just get back on routine next week." Do these sound familiar?

Having your routine thrown off for one or two days can catapult you into a downward spiral that can last weeks and in some cases months if you keep making excuses? Getting derailed is hard, it interrupts our routine. When we take longer than we need to get back on the tracks though, it makes things much worse.

Taking a long time to get back on routine after we have been derailed can put us in a rut or make us have to start all over again because we have lost all the progress we have made. Sometimes it can even cause our goal to take so long that we eventually give up. Derailments can easily look like a perfectly packaged gift in the form of an excuse to "take a break" or "quit" for a while. Be careful to not fall into the "excuse" trap.

Life is fluid and always moving and changing so we need to be adaptable with it. We need to know how to get on and off the track quickly. The best leaders know how to accept derailments and jump right back into their winning routine as soon as possible.

Anticipate Possible Interruptions

I know that it sounds crazy to plan for an interruption, but you can look ahead at your schedule and anticipate more than you realize. Do you have a holiday coming up? Is there a really busy season of work about to take place? Do you have family coming to town to visit?

By looking ahead and anticipating these interruptions you can create a winning game plan ahead of time. If you know that your kid's spring break is next week, then plan ahead and create a strategy that will let you fit your goal into their spring break.

Our schedules are constantly adjusting and shifting, if we want to be productive and succeed we must become adaptable and find ways to still complete the important tasks in our day and focus on the most important things in our lives despite the changes in our schedules.

When life throws you off of routine, staying on track with your goals won't just happen. You have to plan for it and make it happen. Sometimes we have to be creative to fit our goals in, but we can do it.

A couple years ago I had a goal to read one book per month. My plan was to read every evening. With two kids it was rare that I had time to sit and read since the interruptions were endless. Usually by the evening I ended up being so tired that I didn't want to read.

I knew that if I was ever going to reach this goal I was going to have to be creative. So my strategy shifted from reading at night to bringing a book with me everywhere I went.

I realized that I spent a lot of time just waiting in the pick up line at school and I could be reading during that time. I spent hours each week sitting at soccer practice so I started reading then too. Every time I found myself waiting—at a doctor's office, dentist or anywhere—I would just pull out my book and read.

At the end of the year I ended up reading over fifty books, that's over four books per month. We can achieve so much more than we realize if we look ahead and make creative adjustments along the way.

Your Turn

Pull out your calendar and look through the next month. What interruptions and derailments do you see coming up in the next month? Write them here.

Have A Back-Up Plan

It is always nice when plan A works out perfectly for us, but let's be real, how often does that actually happen? You need to have a back-up plan(s) ready and waiting for you so you can make a quick and easy adjustment to your goals when necessary.

An example might be:

I know that Tuesday I have a field trip with my daughter's class so I will not be able to go to the gym like I usually do. So plan A is out for today.

Plan B: Choose to workout at home later that evening after the field trip.

Plan C: Wake up early and workout before we leave for the field trip.

If both plans B and C just can't happen then...

Plan D: I will be sure to get back into the gym on Wednesday and not let myself fall off the wagon just because I missed Tuesday. At least I am getting right back at the gym and not missing two days in a row.

REMEMBER: No Excuses! If you are only willing to work on your goal when all the stars align perfectly then you will never reach it. Have a back-up plan(s) in play.

Your Turn

Use the space below to create a back-up plan for the derailments you wrote about that will happen in the next month. Get detailed and think through each derailment and how you can make adjustments to try and still hit your goals.

On the days that you can't do anything about your goal because the derailment is too big, give yourself grace and let it go that day. It's ok, you don't have to be perfect, but make sure you have a plan to get right back at it the next day.

Get An Accountability Partner

If no one knows about your non-negotiables, when you get stressed out, derailed or overwhelmed your routine easily stops. We need accountability in our lives to help keep us on track. Without accountability we don't just fall off the wagon more often, but we tend to stay off a lot longer because no one is there to remind us to get back on.

How can we be expected to stay true to the Five Non-Negotiables in our life without the occasional encouragement, shoulder to cry on or hug from a friend that lingers just long enough that we literally feel our heart swell?

No one is meant to do life alone. We need each other, especially like minded, driven, encouraging people. If you keep getting derailed, then get an accountability partner. We need others to cheer us on, hold us accountable and push us towards our dreams.

Your Turn

It is time for you to stop trying to reach your goals alone. Think about who you could ask to become your accountability partner. This could mean having a short call once a week to check in with you or sending weekly text reminders. Use the space below to write the name of the person you will ask to be your accountability partner.

You Can Master Getting Back On Track

Speaking of derailments, when I finally started healing after my surgeries and getting back at the gym it wasn't long until Covid hit! This time though I did not let myself stay off track. I changed my plan from going to the gym everyday to working out in my garage. I didn't have a whole lot of equipment, but I had enough to get my heart rate up and build some strength.

It was hard motivating myself to workout alone in my garage. It was hard to come up with unique exercises with only a few pieces of equipment. But I came out of quarantine healthier than I started it and I am now building on that.

Let's stop complaining and making excuses and getting stuck when our train falls off the tracks and let's realize that life is full of interruptions, but we can get back on tracks quickly and keep going.

If you have struggled with getting back on the tracks in the past, push that aside and start fresh today. You can change your habits and you can become an expert at getting back to your routine quickly.

All Or Nothing Mentality

There is one last thing I want to address in this chapter and that is the, "all or nothing mentality."

When I had the two unexpected surgeries I wish I could say that I just jumped right back in the gym as soon as possible, but the truth is I pretty much gave up on exercising completely until I could go back at full strength.

When the doctor told me that I wouldn't be able to workout hard for at least six weeks, I didn't see the point in working out at all before the six weeks were up. If I can't go hard in my workouts, then why workout at all?

This is what I call the "all or nothing mentality" and it is a losing mentality.

I know that rest and recovery is extremely important after a surgery and I am not taking away from that, but I took it beyond the "essential rest" and entered into excuses and lazy mode. Since I couldn't do everything at 100% I gave up on most things. This mentality caused me to hit the reverse button in many of the goals that I had worked so hard on.

I would not have lost nearly as much muscle or strength if I had simply walked on the treadmill or did small exercises that would not affect my recovery during those six weeks. When I finally went back to the gym I had weeks of work just to catch up to where I had already been a few months before.

There are many times in life that we can't be "all in" on our goals or routine. If we are stuck with an all or nothing mentality then we will end up either procrastinating in our goals for years because we never feel we can be all in so it is never the right time to start, or we will keep starting, but as soon as a setback comes our way we will give up and go back into reverse until we can be all in again.

This mentality limits you. It gives you only two options... All or Nothing. When the world is full of endless options and possibilities, don't limit yourself to only two possibilities. Be flexible and open to the possibilities around you. Sometimes when we have to slow down, adjust or re-think the way we do things.

You have spent a lot of time and energy with this book creating a routine that will help you win in life. The longer you stay off that routine, the longer it is going to take you to win. The goal is not to have the perfect life where we never get derailed, the goal is to minimize the amount of time the derailment keeps us off the tracks.

My daughter Jordyan used to love playing with her train sets. She would spend hours building tracks from the game room down the stairs, through the halls and around the kitchen island.

She would always come and get me when a track was completed and wanted me to watch the first time she attempted to have the train go on the tracks. We would countdown from ten and she would let the train go. Most of the time it wouldn't be long before the train fell off the track because she had made the tracks turn too sharply or an incline too steep and the train couldn't make it.

I always felt so bad for her in those moments because she would literally take two days building just one course. She would spend hours trying to develop these elaborate tracks and in a matter of seconds her plan failed.

While I was sitting there feeling sad for her, she taught me an amazing lesson. She picked up the train and said in her little girl voice, "Oh no, the train fell off the tracks, but I can fix it." And just like that she went back to adjusting and fixing the track.

She didn't cry and complain and tell me how horrible it was that her well thought out and elaborate plan didn't work the way she hoped. She didn't throw the train in frustration because things didn't go her way. She didn't have time for that because she was so focused on her final goal of getting the train all the way through the course without falling off. Her goal was driving her forward.

This whole process would happen almost every time she built her tracks. After she had spent another fifteen minutes fixing the spot on the track she would come and get me. Once again we would count down from ten and usually within a few seconds the train would fall off again and she would jump right back to it, meticulously fixing each piece of track one by one.

Let's stop complaining and making excuses and getting stuck when our train falls off the tracks and let's realize that we can fix this and get back up and try again.

Your Turn

Do you struggle with an "all or nothing mentality"? What areas of your life do you have an "all or nothing mentality"?

How is this mentality holding you back?

Write out what your new mentality is going to be when you cannot be "all in" on one of your goals.

Non-Negotiable #5

Finances

19

Non-Negotiable #5: Finances

"Those who don't manage their money will always work for those who do."

-Dave Ramsey

If you are like me then you have had a very stressful relationship with money. When bills came due every month, my anxiety would skyrocket. No matter how hard Michael and I worked, there was barely enough to make it and every time we had to have a "money talk" it turned into stress and tears. We couldn't even think about saving for the future, we were just trying to save enough money to have a decent grocery budget each month.

Not only did we struggle to pay the bills, but to be honest we felt completely helpless in knowing what to do about our financial situation. I felt stuck and all the sophisticated financial talk seemed intimidating. It was like a strange language that I would never be able to decipher, especially since I couldn't pass my accounting class in college.

I ended the semester with a D and had to retake the class again the following semester and I barely passed it the second time around.

For years we worked our tails off and slaved away and only scraped by. In fact there were many years we didn't even scrape by, we went into credit card debt. That debt only added to the stress. Money literally became the dictator of our life. Every time we wanted to do something or go somewhere the first question was: can we afford it? The answer was almost always a resounding NO.

Can you relate to my life in any way? Do you feel like your money is running your life instead of you running your life? Do you want to change your financial situation but, like me, feel inadequate to do so?

I know how you feel. But the good news is you actually can do something about your finances. You don't have to give up your dreams of traveling the world, retiring early, giving to that charity or just being able to pay your bills each month without worry and stress.

I am no financial expert, in fact it is hilarious that a girl who almost didn't graduate from college because she couldn't pass her accounting class is even writing a chapter on finances. But hey, that should tell you that if I can change my finances, then so can you.

Your Turn

Do you feel that you have a good handle on your finances?

Is paying your bills stressful for you each month?

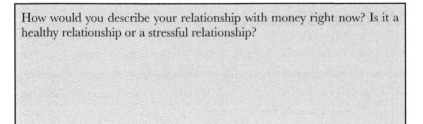

How would you describe your relationship with money right now? Is it a healthy relationship or a stressful relationship?

What's The Problem?

So what was the problem? Why couldn't I manage my money?

The answer was me. I was the problem.

My entire mindset, attitude and spending habits was the real problem. Robert Kiyosaki, the author of *Rich Dad Poor Dad* said, "Financial freedom is a mental, emotional and educational process." Building financial freedom means rebuilding who we are on the inside in relation to money.

You actually don't need to have an accounting degree from Harvard to be a good money manager. Dave Ramsey, the famous personal finance coach says, "Winning at money is 80 percent behavior and 20 percent head knowledge." Meaning the habits we consistently live out with our money is 80 percent of the battle.

I am not going to negate the other 20 percent. Having wisdom and knowledge with your money is also very important, but we have a lot of people walking around with head knowledge about money and they are still in debt because of their spending habits.

Heck, even I, who didn't know the first thing about investing nor a single financial term knew that I should not have been charging things on a credit card, yet I continued to do so. Knowledge does not always equal power, applied knowledge does.

Wrong Mindsets

Our thoughts become our actions. How we think about money is the first step to controlling what we do with our money. Many of these wrong mindsets have become second nature to us and we don't even recognize that they are making our financial decisions for us.

Let's uncover some of these mindsets because they are likely part of the reason you aren't where you want to be with your finances.

Not Being Content

For some reason we think the more money we get, the more things we should buy. I am sure you have heard the quote, "Don't go broke trying to look rich." The moment we make more money we stop being content with the paid off car we already have and we must upgrade to a newer, more expensive car.

John Rockefeller was once asked, "How much money does it take to satisfy a man?" He replied, "Just a little more." Do you catch yourself saying, "Just a little more and then I will be happy?"

We get so hooked on the latest and newest things that when we look at our used possessions we see them as subpar. While there is nothing wrong with wanting nice things, we must first and foremost learn to be content with what we have. If we can't learn to be content, it will be very hard to stay out of debt, or keep from spending our entire lives working ourselves to death for more stuff.

"Keep your lives free from the love of money and be content with what you have" (Hebrews 13:5). Learning to be content is the key to a happy life, not chasing more money. Chase your dreams and manage your money wisely and you will discover you have everything you need.

Your Turn

Do you struggle to be content with what you have?

What area do you struggle the most at being content with?

What is the main reason that you struggle with being content? Do you feel the need to impress others or to keep up with the Jones'?

What is one thing that you could start doing to help you be more content and grateful for what you already have?

Using Money To Find Self Worth

When you gain self-worth from money it is hard to ever get ahead financially because the constant pressure you put on yourself to impress others with your money causes you to spend money that you should be saving or investing.

How much stuff you have or how nice your stuff is says absolutely nothing about your worth as a person. You cannot view money as a yardstick to measure your worth. You need to see money for what it is, a tool to help you achieve your purpose.

Your Turn

Write about a time when you tried to use money to bolster your self-worth.

In what ways do you use money at times to make you feel better about yourself?

We Compare Our Money With Other's Money

We compare our "stuff" against others "stuff" and if our pile isn't as big or nice as theirs, then we think there is something wrong with us and we need to go out and get more stuff. Even if it means charging it on a credit card or working two jobs. We NEED more stuff, nicer stuff.

When we see the social media posts of others going to fancy dinners or nice vacations we start comparing our lives and begin to feel less than. This horrible feeling then causes us to go buy more "stuff" so we can feel better. This vicious cycle will not give you financial freedom.

Your Turn

Who is someone in your life that you compare yourself to financially?

Why do you struggle with comparison with this person?

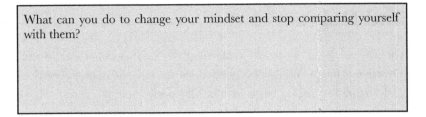

What can you do to change your mindset and stop comparing yourself with them?

We View Money As The Key To Happiness

Money can make life easier and give you more freedom, but at the end of the day money is not your source of fulfillment. If you are unhappy then that is a problem on the inside of you and no amount of external things including money can fix that.

If you keep hearing this little voice in the back of your head say, "One day when I have more money I will finally be happy", then you need to adjust your thinking. You can be happy right now in this moment whether you have a lot of money or not.

Money is a tool to help us fulfill our purpose and living out our purpose is what will bring us great joy, not having a lot of money in a bank account. Money is a tool to help us. It is not the source of anything.

Your Turn

Do you sometimes think that money will make you happy?

How do you use money at times to fill a void of unhappiness in your life?

Bad Habits

The way we spend our money is like most other things in our lives; mainly through our habits. We usually spend about the same amount on groceries, shopping and eating out each month. Of course there are variations, but overall we tend to be creatures of habit and our spending is not immune to habit.

Once something becomes a habit we no longer need to think about it, it is kind of like putting your car on cruise control. The only problem is, for many of us our finances are on cruise control and the destination is taking us is deeper into debt. It is time to take our finances off cruise control and pay a little closer attention to where our money is going.

We just went over some of the wrong mindsets we have towards money that keep us in bad financial positions, now we are going to talk about some of the bad habits we have with our money.

We Focus On Gaining Money, But Not Saving It

It is amazing how hard we will work to get more money and then how frivolous we will be with it once we have it. We spend hours each month trying to gain more money through work, but we won't spend a single minute working on a plan to help us retain the money we earn.

Part of the reason we do this is because we tend to view our money as a source of immediate gratification rather than a nest egg for our future. Instead of planning and budgeting and making our money work for us, we overspend and get into debt and end up becoming a slave to money.

Your money should be working for you, not the other way around. Oftentimes it is not because we don't make enough money that we become a slave to money, it's because we don't spend our money wisely.

I know there are particular situations and circumstances in which you can truly have a real lack of money and it is out of your control. I have been that person before, but I am not talking about that, I am talking about the person who technically makes enough to live, but spends their money unwisely instead.

We have no problem slaving away 24/7 to get money, but then once we finally have it we blow it on impulse purchases forcing us to have to get back to the grind 24/7 again to get more money and the vicious cycle goes on. Then we wonder why we don't have any time to pursue our dreams, we are too busy working to support our habit of bad spending.

Your Turn

Do you have a regular time each month that you spend planning out how you will keep the money you work so hard for?

If not, why not?

We Miss Out On Our Chance To Give

Part of every single person's purpose is to give. Our money is not just a tool to help us, it is also a tool to help others. We should all be giving.

Life is never complete when it is all about us. Without some form of giving in our lives we become one dimensional and selfish. Most people want to give back in some way, they just haven't made the time.

Let me be clear though, it is a sacrifice to give. If you are waiting for a convenient time to give then you will be waiting your entire life. Giving will cost you something and that is part of its beauty, sacrificially setting someone else above yourself.

The Five Non-Negotiables

Being generous is a conscious decision you make. It doesn't just happen and it isn't always easy. That's why so many people go most of their lives thinking about helping others, but never actually doing it. Giving is hard, it forces us to sacrifice, it costs us something.

When I was growing up my dad would always tell me, "With much given, much is required." I used to get so annoyed at that, but as an adult I now see the truth in that statement. We have been given so much in this life and we were not given all this "stuff" and all these "talents" only for our own betterment.

When we give it also helps keep our hearts in check from the love and obsession of money. We don't want to live our lives in love with money, always chasing after it. We want to live our lives fully alive, loving people and chasing after our purpose.

Giving helps us to take our eyes off only accumulating wealth for ourselves and back onto others and that is a powerful part of our purpose. Don't miss out on helping others. Don't be selfish with your money.

Your Turn

When was a time that someone was in need and you selflessly gave to them?

How did that make you feel?

Are you giving and sharing your money and resources with those in need?

If not, is there some organization or person that you would like to be giving to?

We Don't Make A Plan For Our Money

Many people get their paycheck every two weeks and by the end of the two weeks it is completely gone and to be honest, most of us could not recall where all the money went.

You might think you have a general idea, but if you were to really sit down and analyze the numbers you might be shocked to discover that your little $4 Starbucks run once and sometimes twice a day is actually eating about $150 out of your income each month. No wonder you don't have that extra $40 a month for that gym membership.

We can't forget all you Target mamas out there. You go to Target in need of toothpaste and you walk out with a cart full of non-essentials that weren't on your list, but of course it is all super cute stuff. If you do two of those Target runs per month they can easily add up to an extra $200 per month or more.

I am not saying that any of these things are bad. What I am saying is, if you don't know where your money is going every month then that is bad. And I don't just mean being able to give a general idea, I mean actually knowing how much you spend on things, because you control your money and budget it.

It's Time To Make A Change

As you can see we have our mindset and spending habits backwards. Instead of seeing our money as a tool to help us fulfill our purpose it has become a tool used to prove our worth and value. At times, we have used our wealth in every way except the way it is intended to be used.

I am not saying these things to make us feel guilty, I am saying them to help us face our own truths. The world wants to coddle you with a warm bottle of excuses and a blanket of lies. It is time to face the truth about your money and make a change. It's not time to read about making a change, it's time to put your money where your mouth is and make a real actual change in your finances.

There is nothing wrong with money. There is nothing wrong with having a lot of money, driving nice cars and going on shopping sprees. Let's be real clear on the shopping sprees, they are completely acceptable. There is a problem, however, if the shopping spree is going on a credit card because you can't pay for your shopping habit and you are accumulating debt.

There is a problem if your huge sums of money are your source of self-worth or if you hoard it all for yourself and never share with those in need. What I am trying to say is there is a balance when it comes to money and one of the best ways to achieve financial balance is through a balanced budget.

Not taking time to tend to your finances is equivalent to planting a garden and never tending to it. At the end of the season there will be nothing to harvest. At the end of each paycheck do you feel like there is nothing to harvest? If so it is time to start tending to your money: budgeting, giving and being content.

Budgeting

Your money does not go from your bank account into a dark black hole and disappear, and if you feel like it does then you simply have a habit of not budgeting and keeping track of your money. The good news is that you can change today and start budgeting.

Do you remember back a few chapters ago when I was telling you that some of the best financial advice I ever received was from Dave Ramsey? He said, "Spend all of your money on paper each month before you spend it in person." I know we already discussed this in a previous chapter, but that was in regards to budgeting our time. Right now I want to talk about this same lesson in regards to budgeting our finances.

As a review, what Dave Ramsey meant was to look at your upcoming month and anticipate all your expenses and allocate money for each expense until you have spent every penny before the month has even begun.

This means allocate your money for savings, fun, bills, etc and spend every penny on paper. This paper then becomes your spending plan that you will follow for the next thirty days. As long as you stick to the plan you will reach your financial goals for that month. There is no guessing or wondering if you are staying on track.

Your budget will need to adjust each month a little with holidays, vacations, etc…, but for the most part once you have a general budget established that keeps track of your monthly expenses it really doesn't take that long to maintain it.

Your Turn

Do you have a monthly budget?

If you do, do you stick to the budget consistently?

If you don't, why don't you have a budget?

Benefits Of Budgeting

Gives Your Freedom

I know that this idea of budgeting every penny might sound restrictive, but I promise you that it is just the opposite. Sure, taking the time to budget is not necessarily fun, but having total control over your money is incredibly fun.

Being able to pay cash for splurge items and go to sleep each night peacefully because you don't have debt hanging over your head is liberating. Actually taking vacations because you have the self control to save for the trips and being able to buy Christmas gifts with cash without stress is incredible.

Yes budgeting is not the most exciting thing you could do with your time, but it is one of the wisest things you could do with it and it is also one of the most liberating.

Since your finances affect almost every other area of your life, it seems to me like sacrificing a few hours to get a budget together would be worth all the other benefits you will get from it.

Gives You Control Over Your Money

Dave Ramsey summarizes budgeting by saying, "A budget is telling your money where to go, instead of wondering where it went." Once you get in the habit of spending all your money on paper first, you will be in the habit of taking control of your finances and building a life of financial freedom.

Having a budget also makes it a lot easier to say no to impulse purchases because you realize that this impulse isn't in the plan you worked so hard to put together. The decision has already been made for you and now you just have to stick with it.

Budgeting on paper first allows you to allocate where you want your money to go and what you want it to accomplish for you each month. You are taking back the reins and making your money work for you.

Tool To Build Your Future

A budget is one of the number one tools to help you build your financial future: retirement, investments, residual income.

Once you have control over your money through a budget you can start directing your finances towards investment and savings that will help make you truly wealthy and give you a nest egg for retirement and a rainy day.

When you gain control over your money there is no limit to what you can create for yourself with it.

Without a budget it is nearly impossible to have anything left over to save and even if you do, you usually don't know what to do with the leftover money or how to invest it wisely because you are not focused on your finances.

Your Turn

What is one thing that you have always wanted, but have not had enough money to pay for?

If you had more money, how would you like to spend it? Charity, house cleaner, meal delivery service?

What area of your life would you be able to experience more freedom if you had more money?

Money = Options

Having a lot of money sounds great, but why is it so great? Besides being able to afford for someone else to clean your house, which to be honest is about all the information I need to know about having money that makes me think it's the greatest idea ever. But really why is it so important to have control over our finances?

The answer is simple: Money = Options.

Money can give you the freedom of choice. Without money there is no choice of where you want to go on vacation, because there is no vacation. There is no choice of which non-profit organization you want to donate to, because there is no money left to donate. There is not the option of hiring help with your housework so you have more free time with your family or retiring early so you can volunteer at the animal shelter.

So when we give up on trying to manage our finances, when we throw in the towel and say, "well this is just the way life will always be," you aren't just giving up money you are also giving up your freedom. When you neglect and negotiate with your finances you are also negotiating away your choices.

Money is not the answer, it is not magic and it does not give us self worth, but it does give us options. Money is a tool and can be a blessing in our lives when we manage it correctly and keep a pure heart about it.

Don't Tackle This Alone

I am no expert on money or budgeting and I certainly do not claim to be, that's why I got help. Before we hired help I always thought that spending money to help manage my money was a complete waste of money.

I learned a valuable lesson by hiring an incredible financial management company. Within the first two months of working with them we had already saved more than what it cost us for their help for an entire year.

They made us set financial goals, helped us with investments, budgeting and had monthly meetings with us to hold us accountable. They walked us through all the steps for buying stocks, retirement planning and made sure we set up the best college fund for our kids.

We had someone there to hold our hand through the entire process and educate us as well as hold us accountable. It was the best financial investment we have ever made. If you can afford to hire a financial planner, do it! It will more than pay for itself many times over.

Hiring a financial planner is not the only option you have to get help though. Years before we hired a financial planner my husband and I took some of Dave Ramsey's classes. They were very inexpensive and I learned a lot of important lessons about money from his program. There are many other programs like his by other financial experts that you can look into.

You can also read books or listen to podcasts, you don't necessarily have to spend a lot of money or even any money to get more educated on finances. There are free resources all over the internet these days.

For years Michael and I tried to gain control of our finances alone and we kept failing. As soon as we invested in help our finances turned around dramatically. I want to encourage you to make an investment in something that can help you reach your financial goals and hold you accountable along the way. You don't have to do it alone and any money you spend on properly managing your financial future will pay for itself.

Your Turn

There are many forms of help and education out there when it comes to finances. What help are you going to seek? Reading a book, listening to a podcast, hiring a financial company? If you aren't sure yet, stop right now and do some research. Use the space below to write out exactly what help you are going to use to start reaching your financial goals.

Now take the first step towards getting that help. Make a call to the company for more information, order the book or download the podcast. Whatever your first step is, do it now and write, "I am going to start making my money work for me" below once you have done it.

Get Back Up And Try Again

Michael and I have created budgets for our family multiple times and failed again and again to maintain them. They were good budgets too. We took hours planning them out and crunching the numbers, setting us up for complete success and within two months we would completely fall off the bandwagon.

We would get tired or stressed and make excuses to overspend or we would stop making the budget a priority and eventually forget about it and go back to our old habits of spending.

You will probably fail at this several times before you get it right, don't let that discourage you. Get back on track with your budget right away and start again. Eventually following your budget will become a new habit in your life that will set you up big time for success.

Don't let a small failure or hiccup give you an excuse to give up. When you mess up, make the necessary adjustments and keep going. Don't stay derailed for long.

Your Turn

What is the main thing that trips you up the most from sticking to a budget? Stress, emotions, excuses, lack of self-control?

If you mess up on your budget what is going to be your plan to get you back on track?

Don't Negotiate With The Budget

The reason that I am telling you that a budget needs to be non-negotiable in your life is because you will never have financial freedom without it. Having money saved, a good retirement or a paid off house can open doors for you to pursue other dreams.

It is a big shift to start disciplining yourself to stay within a budget, but as you begin to stick with it day in and day out, you are going to end up creating a new habit and before you know it, your spending habits will automatically fit your budget.

The key is you can't quit at the beginning when it is tough, at the beginning when you don't see progress and your emotions are screaming at you to satisfy them with all the shiny stuff around you. Just stick with your budget for a few months and pretty soon you will no longer crave the shopping sprees and you will literally start craving the financial freedom you are achieving.

Having a budget and sticking to it is non-negotiable in your life now.

Creating A Budget

Ok this part is going to take you a while, but it is worth it so be patient. Remember I did not write this book to inspire you to get control of your finances, but never actually do anything about it. You did not pick up this book to be reminded of the things you should be doing all while staying exactly the same.

This book was created to help you start taking action and if you have gotten this far in the book then you obviously are a person of action. So I am asking you right now to take action with your finances. Do the hard things. This is your last non-negotiable so give it your very best effort.

You need to create a monthly budget. If you have never created a budget before then consider using a financial app or doing some research online on how to create a budget.

Budgets are really simple, they just take time because you have to collect records of your monthly income and expenses.

Your Turn

It might take more than one sitting to put your budget together so I want you to pull out your calendar and schedule an exact day and time that you are going to start setting up your budget. Write, "I am good at managing my money and I make my money work for me" below once it is scheduled.

Financial Goals

Now it is time to set a non-negotiable financial goal. Remember the non-negotiables are not about being perfect. The non-negotiables are about taking one small non-negotiable step forward in this area of your life. You don't have to get all of your finances in order at the first try, start with small baby steps.

I normally don't give too many suggestions as far as what your goal should be because this book is about you and your personal life, but when it comes to finances, if you can set a goal to create your budget by a certain date I think that is probably the best goal that you could possibly make right now. If this goal is too much for you then consider something smaller like: eating out one less time per month.

Your Turn

Set a realistic financial goal right now and write it below.

Take some time to write out your why. Why have you created this goal and why are you going to make the necessary sacrifices to stick with it?

It's time to add your financial goal and your why to your phone or wherever you store your goals and whys. When your morning alarm goes off you can review it. Write, "It feels so good to know where my money is going" below once you have completed this.

It might take a few days to complete your budget. Do not allow yourself to get overwhelmed, you need to get your finances under control. Try to carve out as much time as you can right now to complete it. Dragging it out over weeks will make the task feel so much harder than it really is. Sit down and knock this budget out as quickly as you can.

Once you have completed your budget write, "I have a budget and I'm sticking to it" below.

Now that you have a budget it is time to make it non-negotiable. Sign your name below as a promise that you will stick with this budget. This is a deal that you are making with yourself for your financial future.

X_____

You Can Do This!

Even if you are bad at math and bad at numbers and bad at spending, you can do this!

Imagine the joy when your bills arrive in the mail and you are able to pay them without a worry in the world. Imagine your monthly financial talks with your spouse being a celebration of the progress you are making towards your financial goals rather than a huge guilt trip that ends in fighting and tears.

Imagine being excited about looking at your savings account because it has grown larger in the last thirty days. Imagine not only being able to pay your mortgage, but being able to write a check to help pay someone else's.

This can be your life, this can be your reality. You do not have to settle for a life of financial stress and anxiety. You can gain control over your finances. You, yes you who is in debt, or addicted to shopping or knows nothing about money or budgeting. You can have financial freedom.

Your Turn

What is the benefit that you are most excited about from your budget?

I know that you can do this, but I need you to know that you can do this. Write yourself a list of all the reasons why you can stick to your budget.

Financial Books I Recommend

Here is a list of some of my favorite financial books.

For Understanding Money Basics

- *Get Good with Money* by Tiffany Aliche

Learning How To Budget And Get Out Of Debt

- *The Total Money Makeover* by Dave Ramsey

Changing Your Money Mindset

- *Think and Grow Rich* by Napoleon Hill
- *Your Money or Your Life* by Vicki Robin

How To Know Who To Turn To For The Right Financial Advice

- *Stress-Free Money: Overcome These Seven Obstacles to Find Financial Freedom* by Chad Willardson *(also, my amazing financial advisor)*

How To Be Smart With Your Money And Build Wealth

- *Rich Dad Poor Dad* by Robert T. Kiyosaki
- *The Richest Man In Babylon* by George S. Clason

Understanding Investments

- *Unshakeable: Your Financial Freedom Playbook* by Tony Robbins
- *The Intelligent Investor: The Definitive Book on Value Investing* by Benjamin Graham and Jason Zweig

20

Overcoming The Blahs

"That's enough todaying for today."

-Blah

What Are The Blahs?

You know those days when you wake up and you feel blah. You feel like you are in a funk that includes a lack of motivation, energy and drive. You don't want to be disciplined and productive. You want to be indulgent and lazy.

You don't necessarily feel hopeless or depressed, but you don't feel great either. You wake up not quite feeling like your go-getter self. Maybe you didn't get enough sleep, you have strife in the office that is pushing you down or you're getting over a cold. You may not even know why you are feeling this way, but for some reason you woke up with a serious case of the blahs and the thought of negotiating with your non-negotiables is sounding better by the minute.

I don't know why we tend to build up these ideas in our minds that super successful people are motivated all the time. Maybe they are, but I tend to think that the majority of people struggle with motivation.

We assume that if our emotions and motivations are not aligning with what we think we should be doing then there is something wrong with us. We assume that if we don't feel motivated to workout then we should feel guilty about that. This could not be further from the truth.

Doing something even when you don't feel like it just because it is the right thing to do is part of success. Staying consistent with your non-negotiables and positive habits in the face of the blahs is heroism in my book.

It is the days and times that you are not motivated and you still choose to do it anyways that you grow the most. God never asked us to be motivated, He simply asked us to be obedient.

It is important to also state that there is a need for balance. Sometimes we get the blahs and it is time to press through, an opportunity for us to strengthen our willpower and conquer our emotions. There are other times when we are feeling the blahs and it might be a sign to us that we need to rest or possibly take a day off.

Sometimes the greatest cure for the blahs is rest. It is important to listen to your mind, body and spirit and determine what you need. Give yourself permission to rest, just don't give yourself excuses to be lazy.

Your Turn

Are you currently struggling with a case of the blahs?

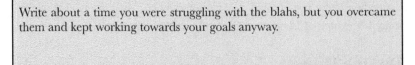

Write about a time you were struggling with the blahs, but you overcame them and kept working towards your goals anyway.

What motivated you to overcome the blahs? How did you do it?

How To Beat The Blahs

One thing I am learning is that it is not enough to just hear about, read about or even know about what you should do, you have to have the ability to actually do it even when you don't want to. It is one thing to know what you should do, but an entirely different thing to do it when your mind and emotions are screaming at you not to.

So how do you overcome negotiating and compromising in the things that matter most in your life? We already talked about how to overcome some of our excuses, but what about when you are in a funk and you really truly just don't want to do it? You struggle day after day and you just can't seem to get on track or find the momentum to stay strong?

It is important that you recognize the blahs when they come on and already have a game plan in place to combat them. It's ok to have off days and down days, but they don't have to completely throw us off or drag us down. If you wait until you are feeling blah to try and figure out how to get out of it, it will be so much harder than simply following a strategy you have already laid out for yourself.

There are hundreds of ways to change your mood and push through times of blah. I am no motivational expert, but I have learned a lot through my depression about overcoming my emotions so here are a few ideas I want to share with you that I hope can help you through your blah times.

Do One Thing

I usually eat a healthy breakfast, but someone in my family who will remain nameless (my Dad) went to one of the best bakeries in Orange County and bought me a pastry this week. A beautiful handmade ooey gooey pastry.

I gave in. I mean, how could I reject such a generous gift from my own father? It was no big deal, just a small splurge. For some reason though, after I ate the one pastry I felt like I had card blanche for the rest of the day to eat whatever I wanted. That one indulgence set me off for an entire day of eating bad.

Has this ever happened to you? One small splurge and you dive straight in a deep spiral down into the abyss. Sometimes one small choice like eating an unhealthy breakfast can trigger us to eat bad all day. As you can tell I am still working on my self-control.

The good news is that the same way that one unhealthy choice can set you in the wrong direction, one healthy choice can set you in the right direction.

If you just can't seem to get on track, if you are feeling blah about every-thing and the thought of aligning your entire day or week to your goals is just too much, then all you need to do is pick one positive thing to do and do it.

For me that usually involves working out or eating a healthy breakfast. For some reason if I can get myself to exercise in some way or eat a healthy bre-akfast, it spurs motivation in me to keep making better choices throughout the day.

The other day I was having a super blah day. I didn't have any motivation and my list of goals seemed too hard. So I looked over my goals and I chose one thing: working out. I bribed myself promising I would only need to workout for ten minutes. The deal was that I only had to walk on the Stairmaster on slow and that I could even watch TV the entire time. I didn't have to push myself, I just had to show up for ten minutes.

After ten minutes on the Stairmaster I was pumped to do more. I ended up spending thirty minutes on the Stairmaster. Then I went over to the weights and lifted for another thirty minutes. After my workout I came back home and felt so good that I sat down and started working on this book and the rest of my day was productive.

If you can force yourself to do one positive thing it just might spur on a chain reaction that leads to a victorious day of overcoming the blahs.

Your Turn

Right now I want you to make a list of the top three things that you are going to do on a blah day to help pull you out of it. You don't have to do all three on a blah day, but the next time you have a blah day then you will be equipped ahead of time with some strategies to overcome it.

You know yourself well, you know what can inspire or push you. Think about what will be easy enough that you can talk yourself into. Below is the space to write your three things.

1.
2.
3.

Have Motivational Inspiration

Sometimes when we are facing the blahs we isolate ourselves and try to dig out of the hole alone. It is important to have encouragement and motivation from others. On days that you just can't seem to find the motivation within, look to others around you for support. There are endless sources of motivation when you need it.

There are certain speakers, videos or TED Talks that I like to listen to that can really kick my butt into gear. When I listen to them they remind me how short life is, how powerful I am and to not give up.

Whether it is a song that pumps you up, an inspiring video that motivates you or a podcast that can propel you towards your goal, it is important to have the resources and use them during times of the blahs.

The great thing about these particular types of motivators is that they don't take much energy to use. Even a person with a severe case of the blahs can sit and watch or listen to something. You can put these on in the car while you are driving to work. Just fifteen minutes of listening can change your attitude for the day. You can put them on while you are working out or in the shower. However you need to do it, just use them.

Your Turn

Make a list of three resources you can use in times of the blahs to help motivate you. Be specific, don't just write, "podcast", write the name of the exact podcast you will listen to. If you aren't sure what podcast will motivate you, then take the time to do some research now to choose the best resources for you. Be sure to download the podcasts or songs so they are quick and easy to access when you need them.

If there is a specific person that you are going to call or text to encourage you on blah days, contact them right now and make sure they know your expectation for their encouragement. Get yourself completely set up so that when a blah day sneaks up on you all you have to do is follow the plan.

1.

2.

3.

Know Your Why

When you get a serious case of the blahs and your motivation is at an all time low, it is time to refocus on your whys. Why should I stay on track even when I am not feeling like it? Why should I make the tough choice when my emotions are all over the place and wanting to quit?

Take a few minutes to dive back into the motive behind the motivation. When motivation is lacking, you have usually lost sight of your motives.

When you know your why- your motive for your actions- it is much easier to stay on track and focused and motivated no matter how blah you are feeling.

For each of your goals throughout this book I have had you write out your why. When you are struggling with the blahs, that is when you need to read through those whys the most. If you are completing all the "your turns" then your whys should already be written and in a place that is easy for you to access whenever you need to.

Tricks To Stick With Your Non-Negotiables

You are not helpless in the fight against the blahs. You can arm yourself with tangible things to help you stay on track, even when you aren't motivated. I have a little bag of tricks that I use to help me stay motivated in my Five Non-Negotiables when I am struggling with the blahs.

As I mentioned before, I basically trick myself into becoming motivated by forcing myself to do just one thing right and that one thing can set off a chain reaction to do another right thing and so on. Even if I only end up doing the one small thing in each non-negotiable that day, I have still made forward momentum and that is a victory.

You can do the exact same thing for your non-negotiables. Create your own bag of tricks to combat against the blahs. You don't just need tips and tricks to help you improve, you need tips and tricks for the down times and hard times, when motivation is lacking.

So we are going to go through each of our Five Non-Negotiables and put together your bag of tricks for each one. This way you will be prepared for the blahs. Don't worry we are going to do this together.

Exercise

What are three things you can do on the days you are struggling to workout because you have the blahs? My list includes going for a walk while listening to a podcast. I know that even on the days I don't want to do anything I can at least motivate myself to walk. I know if I walk around the block listening to someone inspiring, then I will probably end up motivated to do more afterwards.

My list also includes doing ten minutes of exercise. On days that going to the gym just feels too overwhelming then I tell myself all I have to do is ten minutes of exercise and I can be done for the day. Once I start on the ten minutes though, I usually end up finding the motivation to do more. After ten minutes of abs I want to go for a run or start on my goals. It is amazing how that one good choice sets me up for another good choice.

Your Turn

So what are the trick(s) that you are going to use to get moving on the days you are struggling with the blahs in regards to exercise?

Eating Healthy

My bag of tricks in regards to eating healthy includes having a healthy breakfast. For some reason if I start the day out wrong, I find it nearly impossible to get back on track when it comes to food. If I can force myself to start the day out right it really helps me stay on track.

This one might sound weird, but I also have the trick of forcing myself to sit down and watch a clip from a health food show or movie or YouTube video for a few minutes. When I don't feel motivated and I have a case of the blahs, watching television or just wasting time on one of my devices sounds great.

So I will force myself to watch part of a health documentary or something like that. After a few minutes of watching about the effects of unhealthy food on my body I am usually super motivated to change my eating.

Your Turn

What is a trick(s) that you can use to stick to your health goals and overcome the blahs?

Personal Growth

Personal growth for me mostly stems from my relationship with God so making the time to pray and read my Bible is important to me. I wish I could say that because I am a Christian I am always motivated to read my Bible everyday and follow everything it says, but to be honest some days it is a struggle to be motivated to pray and actually apply what the Bible says to my life.

One trick I use to get me motivated to spend time with God is the devotional, "Jesus Calling" by Sarah Young. It is a small little devotional that has a three minute devotion for each day of the year. When I just can't get motivated to pray I tell myself all I have to do is read my devotion today, only three minutes. Once I start reading the devotion I usually can't put it down and find myself opening my Bible and digging deep with God. It is a little trick that has motivated me many times.

For my other forms of personal growth, I will read books or listen to TED Talks or podcasts. On the days that I can't get motivated enough to read, I make the same deal I do with exercise: only ten minutes. I only have to do something towards my personal growth for ten minutes.

The other day I was so unmotivated and I just didn't want to listen to a cheerful podcast so I decided my personal growth time was going to be me journaling about just how unmotivated I was. I was annoyed that I had set this goal for personal growth and I wasn't feel any value in spending my time on personal growth that day so I started writing all about that.

Once I started writing out my feelings, I actually ended up with a lot of insight into my mind and emotions that helped me break through some internal struggles I was having. This insight and breakthrough was totally unexpected. I was just trying to clock in my "personal growth" time so that I was staying consistent in my goals, but by simply showing up I ended up with a major breakthrough.

Being consistent matters, even on the days it doesn't feel like it matters. The magic happens in our lives when we are consistent. There is something that consistency brings to our life that absolutely no other thing can bring. There is no substitute for consistency. Usually the hardest part is just getting started, but once you get going you probably won't want to stop.

Your Turn

What trick(s) are you going to use to help you stay consistent with your personal growth goals on days that you have the blahs?

Financial Management

As you know by now I don't like math, numbers or balance sheets at all. So when I am going through the blahs, one of the first areas I start procrastinating in is staying current with our financial goals. I keep making excuses that I will do it tomorrow and then tomorrow and then tomorrow and so on.

To help prevent myself from procrastination, I tell myself I only have to sit down and review our finances for ten minutes. I set a timer on my phone and force myself to do it. Once I get involved in it though I usually hear the timer go off and keep on working well past the ten minutes.

I also have the trick of forcing myself to walk into my room and stare at my dream board for three minutes. My dream board is the board I made that has pictures of my goals on it. For example, I have pictures of the places I am going to travel with the money we are saving by sticking with the budget.

This board gives me lots of motivation by reminding me of why I am doing the budget in the first place. I tell myself that all I have to do is stand there for three minutes. As I stare at the pictures of the dream vacation places I want to travel to, the SUV I want to have and the home I am dreaming about I usually find myself after three brief minutes excited to sit down and review my budget to make sure I am staying on course financially.

I have even taken a picture of the board with my phone so that I have it with me everywhere I go. When I was trying to decide whether or not to buy a piece of furniture for my house, I literally pulled the board out and stared at my goals and then the furniture. I did this back and forth for a few minutes and finally decided not to buy the furniture now and wait for something more affordable, because that would have eaten into my budget for retirement. I want compound interest right now, not an overpriced piece of furniture.

Well to be honest, I want both. I mean a girl can dream right? One day I believe I will have both, if I stick to my financial plan. This is hard people, I totally get it, I am in this with you right now. But let's finally stick to our financial goals and start living with more financial freedom and less stress.

Your Turn

What is the trick(s) that you are going to use to stay on budget when the blahs are trying to take over?

Family Time

Most often it is busyness and exhaustion that prevents us from family time, but there are times when we are going through the blahs and we just aren't motivated even when it comes to investing in our own families. We hate to admit it, but it doesn't mean we love them any less, it just means we are in a funk and nothing really seems motivating at the time.

There also might be times where there is tension or anger and you don't want to invest in a particular family member due to the friction. Either way it is important to have a bag of tricks to overcome complacency in regards to quality family time.

One of the tricks I use when it comes to motivating myself to spend quality time with my family is I book a few dates with each person on my calendar at the beginning of the month and I tell each person the date and time. Then no matter how I feel I have to be accountable to my commitment. I can't cancel a date with my daughter, I just don't have it in me to let her down like that.

Once we are on the date, I end up having a great time, but sometimes I have to admit I enter these playtimes with little motivation at the beginning. Not because I don't love my kids, but because I am tired and I just want to chill. Let me be clear, I absolutely love spending time with my kids, sometimes I am just so tired, busy or stressed out that it is hard for me to stop and make the time.

Setting up dates ahead of time keeps me focused on the big picture and not the stress of the moment that would rarely allow me to look up and see how extremely important that it is that I take time aside with my kids or husband.

Another trick I use is setting a timer. When my kids are begging me to spend time with them and it really is not a convenient time, I tell them I will play with them for twenty minutes and they know they have my undivided attention for twenty minutes. Once the timer goes off I can go back to my

---

Your Turn

What trick(s) can you use to overcome the blahs and spend quality time with your spouse?

What trick(s) can you use to overcome the blahs and spend quality time with your kids?

---

work, but they had quality one-on-one time with Mommy uninterrupted and I didn't have to feel pressured to play for hours, only twenty minutes. I can do that.

I do this at times when my schedule is packed, but my kids seem like they just need Mommy that day and I am trying to balance multiple things. Days when there is too much to do and not enough time, but my kids need me to make the time. I know I can stop everything for twenty minutes and fill their love tank. We seem to find the time to stop for twenty minutes and scroll through our phones quite often, so I know we can make twenty minutes for our families.

You Are Prepared

Although some of the above tasks may seem trivial, you will be so much more successful at overcoming your blahs if you have already thought ahead about how you are going to overcome them when you face them. Now, you already have a strategy for success before the blahs even show up.

As you grow in motivation and discipline you won't need to use these tricks as often, but it is always nice to have a little bag of tricks in your back pocket to help you overcome the blahs. You never know when they will hit you, but now when they do you will be prepared and armed with some smart strategies to fight them. Just promise me one thing, don't forget to use them.

Personal Letter To The Reader

Dear Reader,

I am so proud of you for reading this entire book, for finishing what you started and not giving up. I know we covered a lot in this book, but I wanted to write you one last message, a letter from my heart to you.

I want you to know that you have the ability to be anyone you want to be. You don't have to stay stuck in any area of your life. If you don't like something about yourself, you can change it. I don't care how many years you have been stuck and how many times you have tried to change and failed.

Start again, try again. You can change. The goal is not perfection, the goal is to be able to look back each year and say, "I'm ahead of where I used to be."

Now is the time to take full responsibility for your life. Take the reins back and start becoming that amazing person that you know you are capable of being.

This is your one life.

You don't get a redo.

The life you want is completely up to you. Your circumstances, financial situation and your past failures, they don't matter nearly as much as who you choose to be.

Trust me, once you make the changes you need and become that strong, confident and consistent person that you know is inside you, there won't be a single thing on this earth that will be able to stop you from reaching your goals and living your life with deep purpose.

Don't look outside of yourself right now, look inside and choose to make the necessary changes. It is who you are on the inside that determines your life.

This is not rhetoric, this is truth.

I care about you deeply and I want the very best for you. I know you can do this.

I wish I could be there with you right now as you are working on your goals to encourage you in person. I believe in you so much.

You are capable of change.

I pray that this book was a blessing to you and helped you make some of the changes you needed in your life. I pray that these changes will go on to affect your entire family and friends for generations to come.

I love hearing from people who have been helped through this book so if that is you then please send me an email to support@chelseadischinger.com and tell me all about it.

I am cheering for you always,

Chelsea

Acknowledgements

First and foremost I want to thank God for putting this message in my heart. It is through your Word that I have learned who I am and what my purpose is. Writing this book has brought me closer to you and the closer I get to you, the hungrier I get for more of you. When I was in my deepest depths of despair of depression I learned that the Footprints poem is actually not a poem, but a true story, because it was then God that you carried me. I give the glory to you for every good thing in my life.

I want to thank my husband, Michael Dischinger, who has supported me in my dream of being an author. You have taken the kids out on adventures so I could write in peace and quiet. You have graciously been willing to spend whatever money that has been necessary to get this book published. You have patiently listened to me talk about this book for hours on end. You have been my rock and support through this process. I am so grateful that you are my husband. Thank you for loving me so well, without you I could never be who I am today.

I want to thank my kids Jordyan and Reese.

Jordyan, I love you with all my heart. You made me a mother and you changed my life for the better. Your strength and courage inspires me to be brave and do big things. Your hugs are one of the sweetest blessings on this earth. Your pranks and sense of humor have helped me laugh through the tough times. Thank you for supporting my dream of being an author and discussing the content of this book over and over with me so I could process it.

Reese, you have been so encouraging during this entire process of writing. You are always telling me that I can do it and how proud you are of me. Your sweet and kind heart is so beautiful and I absolutely love being your mother. You bring so much peace to our home and spending time with you refuels my heart. I have cherished the moments during this process of writing this book when I would look up from my keyboard and see you typing away on your own book that you were writing. Keep dreaming big girl, I love you.

To both my girls, thank you for giving me the time and space I needed to write this book. There were several nights where dinner was a random modge podge of leftovers in the fridge because I didn't have time to cook because I was writing. You never complained, you kindly ate it while I was looking and then ran to the pantry to sneak some snacks when I wasn't looking! Yes I saw you trying to hide those GoldFish crackers from me. Keep loving big and keep dreaming big. There is a whole world out there, go get it!

To my dad Randy LoFranco and my mom Laurie LoFranco, you guys have always believed in my dreams since I was a little girl.

Dad, you taught me to be strong and never give up. In life you don't often get to choose your kids, but you did and you chose me. When you married mom, you loved me as if I had always been your own. That makes me feel like the most special girl in the world.

Thank you for the countless things you have done for me to help me get my book done. From making dinner and bringing it to the house, to taking the girls to their activities so I had extra time to write, to listening to me talk about my book over and over during one of our breakfast dates. You have supported me through every step of this process and I am so grateful.

Mom, you have been a constant cheerleader for me my entire life. Your love has been fuel to my dreams and your support has helped me to never give up. Thank you for all the phone calls you answered while you were trying to juggle your busy work day just so I could talk your ear off about ideas for this book or read you paragraphs from new chapters I was writing.

Thank you for reading the same chapters over and over again to help me get them just right. You have been so patient and supportive through this entire process. Thank you mostly for being an incredible example of a strong powerful woman who goes after their dreams. You have shown me what is possible. I love you so much.

Justin LoFranco my brother, thank you for all of your support and words of encouragement throughout this process. You have listened patiently as I talked your ear off about this book on many of our breakfast dates.

Thank you also for getting my butt back into the gym. Joining the CrossFit community ended up being a huge part of my healing and restoration from my depression. It was exactly what I needed and I never would have done it had it not been for your generous financial and emotional support. Thank you for pushing me. I am so grateful that God gave me a brother like you. I love you.

Jessica Danger, not only have you been my editor, but you have also been my friend. The first time we met this book was only a figment of my imagination. It was Thanksgiving and we sat outside by the firepit and chatted for hours. After finding out that you had published a book, were a professor at a University as well as a mom and CrossFit coach I instantly thought you were one of the coolest people I had ever met.

I shyly mentioned that I wanted to write this book and you encouraged me to stop dreaming and start writing. This book would never have been completed without you. Thank you for all the prayers, coffee dates, texts of encouragement and hours you spent reviewing and editing my book. We have now become good friends and I think that makes me much cooler by osmosis.

My cousin Angie Mancino, thank you for always being there for me. Everytime I called with a new idea for this book or had a new chapter that I wanted to get your opinion about, you patiently listened and offered me your advice and wisdom. Even when you were having a busy day you would pick up the phone and be my support. I love you so much and I am so thankful for you.

Kevin Bjorklund, towards the end of editing this book I really stalled out. I became overwhelmed and stuck. Thank you for kicking my butt back into gear and speaking the truth into me that I needed to hear. You generously volunteered your own time to meet with me for several weeks to push me over that last hump. You believed in me and you forced me to believe in myself. Thank you for giving your time to help my dream come true.

My friend Tiffany DeBoer, you are a supermom. Despite the fact that you have a job, four kids and your own business, you made the time to help me complete this book. Thank you for all the hours you spent reading through my manuscript and sending me your feedback. This book needed your wisdom and advice. I am so grateful for you.

Mike and Mary Dischinger, you are the very best in-laws that a girl could ask for. Thank you for all of your love and support through this process. Thank you for helping pick up the girls from school or driving them to gymnastics so I would have extra time to work on this book. Thank you for your emotional support and love through this process. You guys are a special gift in my life and I am so grateful for both of you.

Jen Hauger, our relationship started out as business, but after meeting you for the first time I knew we would be friends. You have been my incredible photographer for my blog and social media and now for my book cover. Thank you for always making me look so good! When I am feeling shy and insecure in front of the camera you make me feel beautiful and confident. I don't know how you do it, but you have a way of easing my nerves and bringing out a real genuine smile from me.

Chelsea Pagnini, you my friend are such an inspiration. I have loved watching you completely transform your life, health, habits and mindset these past several years. Your dedication and consistency is constantly challenging me. You are living out your purpose and dreams in such a beautiful and passionate way.

Spending time with you makes me better and I am so grateful for who you are and for your friendship. Thank you also for doing my makeup for this book cover. It was an honor to have someone as talented as you work their magic on me. You made me feel beautiful.

Heather Davis, you have been such a huge part of helping me execute all the ideas in my head. For every idea I have you always come back with, "Let me show you how to do that." If it wasn't for you I would still be stumbling in the weeds of my "to-do" lists struggling to figure out how to make all of this happen.

I cannot thank you enough for all the coffee dates where you taught me how to make my dreams a reality. You are such an incredible wife, mother, woman and friend. I appreciate you and I am so blessed to have a friend like you in my life.

Tyler Carroll, thank you for taking me on as a client and designing my cover as well as formatting this book. You have taught me so much about the publishing industry and walked me through the final steps of making this book a reality. I cannot thank you enough for being so generous with your time. I knew nothing about publishing a book on our first call and you patiently walked me through every step. Thank you so much for being a very important piece in making my dream a reality.

References

4: Goal Setting

1. Sage Journal: Behavioral and Cognitive Neuroscience Reviews: The Interface Between Emotion and Attention: A Review of Evidence from Psychology and Neuroscience: By: Rebecca J. Compton from https://journals.sagepub.com/doi/abs/10.1177/1534582303002002003?_cf_chl_jschl_tk_=9VukV7spowhDDnqp0Ve4fbTCR_MEbdDjzpM3moXC1f0-1639509293-0-gaNycGzNCL0

6: Non-Negotiable #1: Review Your Goals Daily

1. Luciani, J. (2015). Why 80 Percent of New Year's Resolutions Fail. Retrieved from https://health.usnews.com/health-news/blogs/eat-run/articles/2015-12-29/why-80-percent-of-new-years-resolutions-fail

8: Habits

1. *The Power of Habit: Why we do what we do in life and business* by Charles Duhigg

10: Non-Negotiable #2: Health

1. https://www.everydayhealth.com/diet-nutrition/poor-nutrition-in-us-poses-threats-to-health-national-security-and-economy-panel-says/

11: Get Off The Hamster Wheel

1. www.yourdictionary.com

12: Mindset

1. *Switch on Your Brain* by Dr. Caroline Leaf

2. The Heart Math Institute: You Can Change Your DNA https://www.heartmath.org/articles-of-the-heart/personal-development/you-can-change-your-dna/

3. AI Commons: Local and Non-Local Effects of Coherent Heart Frequencies on Conformational Changes of DNA: By Dr Rollin McCraty PHD https://appreciativeinquiry.champlain.edu/educational-material/local-and-non-local-effects-of-coherent-heart-frequencies-on-conformational-changes-of-dna/

4. HuffPost: How Your Thoughts Change Your Brain, Cells and Genes: By Debbie Hampton https://www.huffpost.com/entry/how-your-thoughts-change-your-brain-cells-and-genes_b_9516176

5. Be Brain Fit: Do Brain Cells Regenerate? Yes, And You Can Help By: Deane Alban https://bebrainfit.com/brain-cells-regenerate/

6. The Nerve Blog: How You Can Make Quantum Mechanics Actually Work For Your Brain https://sites.bu.edu/ombs/2012/02/21/how-you-can-make-quantum-mechanics-actually-work-for-your-brain/

About The Author

Chelsea is a wife and mother of two amazing girls. She is a speaker, author and the founder of the blog www.chelseadischinger.com whose goal is to help women find their purpose and live it fully.

Chelsea battled postpartum depression for six years. At her lowest point she knew she either needed to make a change right then or she would completely lose herself. Chelsea chose to change and worked for years to transform her mindset, habits, routines and beliefs to become the strong confident woman that she is today.

Chelsea is able to speak to women who have deep struggles and pain and help them to find their way out. Chelsea is known for her tough love approach. Her teachings are full of the same tips, tricks and habits that she used in her own life to overcome her battle with depression.

As a regular guest on podcasts, Chelsea's simple strategies are helping women all over to break free from their past and move forward into their purpose. If you are about to read this book, then get ready to be challenged because Chelsea won't back down until your life is changed.

Made in the USA
Las Vegas, NV
22 November 2022

60024819R00167